'Andrew Douglas-Home and his family [are identified]
with Tweed, perhaps the most glori[ous river] in
which its salmon contribute mightily [. . . No-one is]
better qualified than the author to write about fishing, wildlife
and the wondrous flow of sparkling water across the Borders.'
Sir Max Hastings

'Delivered in more than 50 short, shard-like chapters,
[*A River Runs Through Me*] is considerably more than
the sum of its parts . . . The joie de vivre that this nicely
idiosyncratic book exudes makes it memorable.'
David Profumo, *Country Life*

'An absolute delight… [Andrew Douglas-Home]
is a born writer . . . *A River Runs Through Me*
is unlike any other fishing book I know.'
Tom Fort

'The perfect fishing companion . . . his book is a delight.'
Jeremy Paxman

'It is a love letter not just to the river, but to the
rhythms of family life by its banks. Warm, witty,
and in parts, deeply moving . . . Uplifting.'
Scottish Daily Mail

'Unlike any other fishing book I know . . .
An absolute delight to read.'
Trout & Salmon

'Douglas-Home writes with ease, good humour
and honesty about his fishing and also reflects on
his childhood, education, life and family. Much of
it is touching, and some of it deeply affecting.'
The Field

A
RIVER
RUNS
THROUGH ME

A RIVER RUNS THROUGH ME

A LIFE OF SALMON FISHING IN SCOTLAND

ANDREW DOUGLAS-HOME

Elliott&Thompson

First published 2022 by
Elliott and Thompson Limited
2 John Street
London WC1N 2ES
www.eandtbooks.com

This paperback edition published in 2023

ISBN: 978-1-78396-701-8

9 8 7 6 5 4 3 2 1

A catalogue record for this book is available from
the British Library.

Typesetting by Marie Doherty
Printed by CPI Group (UK) Ltd,
Croydon, CR0 4YY

MIX
Paper | Supporting
responsible forestry
FSC® C171272

For Jane, my (in case you do not have the Latin)
without which not

Contents

Foreword

I hope you will forgive me for beginning what is a very personal memoir that is largely about fishing with a cricket analogy: this part is a bit like opening the bowling, sending down three long hops, a half volley and two full tosses – all of which are duly dispatched to or beyond the boundary by the odious batsman (all batsmen are odious). At which point the skipper will say, 'Thank you, mate', while pointing to the long-leg boundary, where you spend the rest of the afternoon contemplating the unfairness of life.

Non-swanks, that never happened to me, but then the cricketing world is familiar, safe ground. I know how to behave. I have no such experience with the world of books, or 'authoring' as Jeremy Clarkson would no doubt call it. If the long grass awaits what follows, so be it. I will have failed to bowl the one that pitches just short of a length outside the off stump, shapes into the (still odious) batsman and then cuts away off the pitch – the perfect unplayable ball. 'Twas ever thus.

I have no idea how this book happened. An accident of time and place, it was meant to be all about fishing, mainly of the salmon variety. Somehow it has become a wider memoir with the Tweed, my family, and my home in the Borders as the backdrop. I hope both the personal memories and fishing bits form an interesting, even amusing, melange into which you might care to dip every now and then, if only in the smallest room in the house.

Salmon fishing is divided into the usual four seasons, although in the coldest months we cannot catch the silvery beauties – unless you live on the Tay, where they seem to think that fishing from 15 January is sensible; it isn't. I tend to think of my own life as taking a similar shape: the youth of spring, the lively abundance of summer and the gentle decline of autumn leading into our final chapter, winter. It seemed appropriate for this book to follow the same pattern with a degree of latitude when it comes to precise dates.

I hope you will enjoy these memories, even, or perhaps especially, the sad ones. The best is at the end, so even if the others leave you unmoved, do read the last. It is by my wife Jane about our son Freddie. In almost every way the circumstances of his death have defined our lives. It sits at the end of winter, for he was born on 13 December and never made it into spring. As you will realise, she writes far better than me but is too modest to acknowledge it.

If I can become angry about anything, it is about what we humans have done to that most beautiful and noble of fish, the Atlantic salmon. If anyone ever risks giving me a soapbox, I shall give it to you straight between the eyes: we have trashed the place and our salmon are the fall guys. I view my life as a failure in many ways but, so far at least, the biggest is the continuing decline in numbers of a fantastic fellow creature.

In my dotage, and to pass the time in those horribly dark winter evenings, I confess to watching such mindless entertainment as *Escape to the Country* and *A Place in the Sun*, where the prospective buyers, on stepping out onto the patio or decking, routinely say, 'Oh, I can see myself sitting out here on a nice summer's evening with a glass of wine in my hand!' If what follows provides you with a little balm, some peace and calm, a brief escape from the seemingly endless worries of this troubled world, maybe with a comforting glass of whisky or wine in hand, that is all I could possibly ask.

Andrew Douglas-Home, 2022

SPRING

Life began for me on 14 May 1950 at Galashiels in the Scottish Borders, and my spring ended when I was thrown out of Christ Church, Oxford, at the age of twenty. Despite that unhappy ending, I look back on it now as a golden age, just as both the meteorological and piscatorial annual equivalents are equally glorious. The spring salmon season begins in February and runs to the end of May. There is nothing as perfectly beautiful as a spring salmon straight from the sea, or as fresh and sparkling as our beech leaves as they first emerge from their winter sleep in late April. What follows, with some authorial licence as to the precise meaning of spring, either took place in the spring months or sets the scene to my own childhood and my family's life.

My education consisted of Miss Clark's in Darnick in the Scottish Borders, Aysgarth School in Yorkshire, Eton, a gap year, and then Christ Church, Oxford. Throughout it all for this fishing-mad boy there was the constant, magnetic pull of the Tweed. Initially it was just Upper Pavilion, then both Upper Pavilion and the Lees. I would sometimes fish one in the morning and then travel the twenty miles downstream to the other in the afternoon. By the time my father sold Upper Pavilion in 1978, I had revelled in nearly twenty years of the greatest possible fishing pleasure on its dozen or so pools. I knew every stone, every ripple and eddy rather better than I knew the back of my hand. Kind friends have asked me back once or twice since. How I love it.

When not casting on home waters, we used to go to other 'family' beats.* We went to Carham (my mother) on Tuesdays every week, and then there were frequent other visits to Birgham Dub (my father) and to Middle Mertoun (my father's cousin). Shamefully

---

* Stretches of river.

we took it all for granted, as we did the sheer numbers of fish in the 1960s. It was the zenith of Tweed spring salmon fishing. None of us ever dreamed it would end.

That it did come to an end should not be a surprise. After all, historically, periods of spring dominance for salmon runs are rare, so that although I was brought up to think of large numbers of spring fish as the norm, it was, in fact, very much the exception. Logically, it is mad for a fish that eats nothing once it enters fresh water to come into the river in February or March, when it will have to stay there for another seven or eight months, food free, until it is ready to spawn. Sadly, but unsurprisingly, there has been no real sign of any resurgence in spring salmon numbers for fifty years now. They have a hard enough life anyway; much more sensible to come into the river in summer or autumn, with the famine then lasting only a few weeks.

As for now, those springers are like gold dust or priceless gems: rare, most beautiful and much prized.

Upper Pavilion

We lived on a little farm called Easter Langlee. My father was a gentleman farmer and he owned the Upper Pavilion beat of the Tweed: a mile and a half of double bank, and a succession of glorious streamy pools, none too long, endless variety, starting with Galafoot and ending with Kingswellees.

Upper Pavilion might not be one of the champagne beats, but its pools – Carryweil (pronounced *Carry-wheel*), the Narrs (*Noirs*), Brigend (*Brig-end*) and Kingswellees – have a long and distinguished literary history. In his *Days and Nights of Salmon Fishing in the Tweed*, William Scrope (1772–1852) nearly fell into Carryweil as the wading was so bad – it still is 170 years later. He played and lost three mighty salmon and captured only two small grilse* in the Narrs. His incompetence was much to the disgust of his attendant, who, when he tried to grab the rod, ended up being kicked.

My mental scrapbook of memories includes a posse of four salmon following my lure, an upstream minnow, right to my feet in Galafoot, none of them with their mouths open; landing a 15-pound salmon on a fly in a tiny pot at the very top of Carryweil, so high up in the white water that nobody would normally think of even fishing there; losing a huge salmon in the tail of Carryweil after twenty minutes of making no impression on it at all (one of only two or three in my life that I ever thought of as portmanteau size); trying to stand upright in the sweeping rush of water and moving gravel underfoot in the Narrs (worth the risk, as in the 1960s it was the best place); the first 20-plus-pounder caught,

---

* Salmon with only one winter at sea behind them.

with my father hanging onto my wader straps, in a big water in November 1966, thinking I would never get it in; catching a fierce, vicious-looking, tartan be-kyped* 20-pound cock fish in rank summer level conditions† in October 1969 in the Quarry Stream, and swearing it growled at me as I pulled it onto the gravel; and, lastly, the Kingswellees, where we subconsciously lengthened the cast as we approached the boundary, hoping to catch the one that could be lying just over there, at the extremity of reach (it never was).

Upper Pavilion was a stunning and secretly prolific bit of river – in 1966 we caught well over 600 salmon there – and Easter Langlee was a lovely place to be brought up. I was sad when my father sold it, but by then Galashiels was expanding. Fifty years later our old house is in the middle of a massive housing estate, and I have to summon all my powers of recall to think of it as it was. The river is now surrounded on both sides by modern houses and the noise of traffic – progress, some would say, but not for me and my treasured memories. I still wish my father had not sold it – he had his financial reasons no doubt and my parents were moving to an even more lovely place at Westnewton in the Cheviots – but I cherish the memory of waking every morning and knowing the day ahead would contain unknown fishing excitements, and that it was all mine if I could just keep my pesky brothers out of the way.

Don't feel sorry for my brothers. I see from my fishing book that the day I caught that 23-pounder in Elwynfoot in 1966, Simon caught seven salmon elsewhere, and over 100 salmon in total that year. Ugh! Elder brothers.

---

* Adult male salmon turn from silver to a darker colour often referred to as tartan; the kype is the lower jaw extension that grows on cock fish when they begin to mature.

† When the water is both low and warm.

A Most Deprived Childhood

For some reason, this particular June weekend sticks out. At just sixteen years old, I could hardly sleep for the anticipation of catching something in those pools, just a field's walk away from the house. The use of the word 'deprived' is entirely ironic.

I was cruelly cast out from my Borders home at the age of eight to an educational institution called Aysgarth near Bedale in Yorkshire. From there I progressed at thirteen to another institution near Slough in Berkshire, in order to further said education. This upmarket prison banned all phone calls home and hardly ever allowed you out, let alone home, except for some curious anomaly called 'Scotch leave' for us northerners, an extended mid-term break. Heathrow was a taxi ride away and those excellent Britannia aeroplanes with their four propellers, the workhorse of the then BEA fleet, whisked me and my younger brother safely to Turnhouse airport at Edinburgh sometime during the late afternoon of Friday, 10 June 1966.

We were collected by our parents and piled into the back of their Morris Oxford motor, our sparse luggage stowed in the boot, and driven to the family home, an hour to the south. Excitement was high with news that there were fish about.

Upper Pavilion is the least well known of the Pavilion beats, but in the 1960s it was by some distance the best. My father let it intermittently and only to family friends in the autumn; his poor deprived sons could fish there whenever we wanted. It was a short walk to the river from the house, essential for a sixteen-year-old in pre-driving days.

The forecast was fine for the whole long weekend and the river low, so success might be had both early and late in the day.

After a quick dinner, we wadered up and got into the Morris Oxford again, with rods protruding from every window, drove round to Lowood House and down to park by the Brigend, the best pool, right on the riverbank, intending to fish until it was dark. My fishing book says I caught one in the Glassweil of 8 pounds with the comment, 'Fine evening, light east wind, caught at 9 p.m., 4 more caught, a few about.' So back to bed, with happy dreams of the day being taught Latin by Nigel (to us inevitably 'Hattie') Jacques near Slough in the morning and a salmon landed in Scotland in the evening. The family catch: five for the day.

I was up and out of the house, booted and rodded, at 6 a.m. as Mrs Donaldson (the incomparable cook – note how *deprived* we were) arrived, with instructions to be back home for breakfast at 8.30 a.m. Down through the lambing field in front of the house I went, over the Melrose to Galashiels road, on down to the Tweed and waded over the tail of the Brigend to the other side. With time short, I did the Narrs and the Brigend, a salmon landed in each, hid them in the long grass for collection later, and waded back over the river, home for a very happy breakfast, with tales of triumph to relay to parents and siblings. My book records catching two more salmon later that morning in the Kingswellees, the most downstream pool, to which I was sent as penance for the earlier pre-prandial success. My book says, 'Caught 4; 15, 11, 7 and 7 pounds; light east wind, 2 before breakfast, 2 caught by others; very good for mid-June.' The family catch: six salmon for the day.

Sunday, purgatory for fishing-mad, time-limited boys, was spent lounging about, maybe indulging in some croquet or cricket on the lawn (more deprivation) while cursing that Scotland should loosen up and allow Sunday fishing, like its Sassenach neighbour.

Up early on Monday, a better fishing day, not so sunny, and I caught three before breakfast in Carryweil, Glassweil and Brigend, with three more later in the day at Kingswellees (one) and Glassweil (two). Astonishingly, elder brother Simon (on his gap year) caught six in Carryweil, my father also managing to catch one when he got anywhere near the water. My book says, 'Caught 6: 8, 8, 8, 7, 6 and 5 pounds; extraordinary for mid-June; 3 before breakfast.' The family catch: thirteen salmon for the day.

Then back into the Morris Oxford, up the A68 to Turnhouse airport, landing at Heathrow late evening, taxi back to school, in bed by 10 p.m. with happy and glorious memories of twenty-four fine salmon caught by the family in barely two full days' fishing. And what next for tomorrow? More Latin, some History and Spanish, then cricket on Upper Sixpenny in the afternoon.

How lucky we were. At the time did we realise? Of course not.

'Where do you fit in? Which one is your father?'

My earliest memory of my father on the river is of him hanging onto me while fishing the impossible wading that is Carryweil. Much later, I would repay this paternal assistance by rowing him in the Temple Pool at the Lees. His most annoying – and deliberate – ploy was to pretend he had not got a fish on, by not lifting his rod, and see how long it took for his oarsman to notice.

For some reason, we all like to pigeonhole the people we meet. Through most of my seventy-one years, when meeting strangers, the first question has been 'What relation are you to the ex-prime minister?' Not so much now, for it was a long time ago, back in the early 1960s, that 'Sir Alec' became PM. After 'He was my uncle' comes the inevitable follow-up, 'Oh really? Where do you fit in? Which one is your father?'

Which is where it gets tricky. You see, there were uncles Alec (PM, Foreign Secretary, PPS to Chamberlain at Munich, etc., etc.); Henry (BBC birdman of yesteryear); William (playwright viz. *The Reluctant Debutante*, *The Chiltern Hundreds*, *Now Barabbas* and numerous others, court-martialled for refusing to bombard Le Havre); cousins Robin (nearly married two princesses, journalist, author, nightclubber extraordinaire, friend of Frank Sinatra); Charlie (editor of *The Times* under Rupert Murdoch); David, successful banker; Jamie, who trained horses and then wrote about them, and last but not least, my brothers Simon, another successful city type, and Mark, also a newspaper editor and then author.

In short, they all put it about a bit.

My father, younger brother to Alec, Henry and William, though older than George (more of him later), was none of the above, I would explain to my inquisitor. His name was Edward.

Before getting that far, the more knowledgeable stranger would run through the list, and be visibly disappointed when I would say 'No', as the list grew longer of those Douglas-Homes of whom my father was not one. He was a farmer who lived quietly in the Borders, shooting, fishing, playing cricket, happily married and only infrequently, and most reluctantly, moving away from home, and then usually to catch or shoot some hapless fish or fowl.

With this explanation of my father's unexciting normality, said inquisitor would lose interest. 'Poor you', I sensed, being an unfortunate offspring of the only one they had never heard of.

The puzzle, for such it certainly was, even to his children, was Edward being, as his brother William described, 'wholly and extraordinarily lacking in ambition'. He was monastic in his absence of materialism, spending most of his non-sporting days running and pottering about his farm, and by 'pottering about' I mean driving his 'bus' (a Land Rover or equivalent), or watching TV, or reading a book, or scolding his beloved dogs. ('Don't be a bore, Tully!' Tully was the last of his Labradors, inherited by us when my father died and who did nothing to deserve such regular rebukes.)

That was pretty much it, all he did after 1945 (he died in 2006 aged eighty-six) when he returned from three and a half years as a guest of the Japanese in various Burmese prison camps and on that infamous railway. He did not garden; he seldom went for a walk, unless to go shooting or fishing; he did not cut the grass, or chop the logs for the fire.

But he was very obviously content; although initially a smoker, he had no vices, ate little, drank little (not teetotal but almost), would not know how to gamble, never thought about money, and wanted nothing except large quantities of cartridges, 20-pound nylon, a rod and some salmon flies. He kept his 'buses' forever, until they were defeated by rust. His otherworldliness was matched only by the size of his cartridge bill.

The puzzle? Was he born like that or was he changed by waking up every morning for three and a half years in a Japanese camp, never knowing if he would be alive or dead by evening, riddled with malaria and dysentery and increasingly malnourished, not knowing if the war would ever be won and unable to communicate with his family (who thought he was dead)? Did that daily remorseless, punishing, incredibly cruel Japanese attrition, unimaginable to us now, make him like that?

Before being captured in Singapore, he was shot and seriously wounded – some say shot where his heart should have been but wasn't (anatomically speaking at least). Somehow he survived.

When Edward walked into the sitting room at The Hirsel, his family home, on his return from prison camp, his father is reported to have looked up from his newspaper, so overcome was he by the sight of his lost son that he blurted out, 'Ted, where have you been all this time? There are two ducks down there on the Leet, why don't you go and shoot them?' Which my father, all six foot and barely seven stone of him, duly did, thereby giving his aged parent time to gather himself. Palpable raw emotion has never knowingly been a Home family long suit.

Shortly thereafter, in 1946, Edward married my mother, prompting his brother Henry to tell us all later, 'Poor Edward, three and a half years in a Japanese prison camp and married the first girl he came across when he got back!' There might be rather more truth in them having met when their fishing lines became

13

entwined, when one was fishing at what is now Lower Birgham on the Scottish side of the river, and the other at Carham on the English side.

After the horrors of war and prison camp, sufficient for a life-time, was just being alive, enjoying his home with his adoring and attentive wife, luxuriating in the glorious freedom of the Borders countryside, in pastimes he loved, with his dogs, his children, then his grandchildren and in the most comfortable surroundings, enough? He must have dreamed of such a life for nearly four years away and in captivity. The only time I saw him visibly shaken was in the 1990s when he heard that the British doctor who had kept them all alive, with almost zero resources, had died.

It would take too long to explain that to those strangers; not famous or infamous like all those other Douglas-Homes, but were any of them as contented, or as deserving of contentment?

Whatever his apparent lack of earthly achievements, he was right up there with the others in the merit stakes. Maybe even more so. My father, the one you haven't heard of. Edward.

Currarevagh

One of the unsolved mysteries of life is the passage of time, and how it rushes by as our allotted span on this earth begins to run out. Yet when we are young, time seems to stand still, especially in those interminable summer holidays from school.

My parents used to take their three over-energetic boys fishing in the summer, once we had outgrown the charms of the peerless beach at Bamburgh and the delights of staying with the Misses Dixon at North Raw, looking over the castle, the nesting fulmar petrels and the cricket ground. When we were sunburned, seemingly all the time, cooling pink calamine lotion was applied in vast quantities. We caught shrimps in the pools by Bamburgh's Stag Rock, about the only reason for which my father would deign to come and join us. He otherwise stayed at home quoting 'the harvest' as his reason for absence. My mother loved Bamburgh, adored sitting in the sun, the beach, the whole place and, had she outlived my father, she might have moved there. There was a blacksmith (there were blacksmiths in every small town in the 1950s) called 'Glamour' and, shockingly, my mother and her friends would titter and giggle whenever they saw him.

The summer fishing trips started with Connemara on the Irish west coast, for two weeks in the second half of August. My mother went along with all this fishing. Despite catching two salmon over 30 pounds in the same week at Carham, where she was brought up, she hardly fished after her marriage. I now have recurrent guilt. Outnumbered four to one by male fishermen, her life was one of self-sacrifice, always putting the enjoyment of the men in her life before her own. She had been a fine horsewoman before we came along, but gave that up when none of us showed any interest. One by one a pony called Twinkle threw us off and ended her equestrian ambitions for the family.

Travelling to Connemara was no easy matter in the early 1960s: load up the Morris Oxford estate, drive over to Glasgow, have the car winched onto the overnight boat to Dublin, and arrive early the next morning by the River Liffie – 'whiffy' Liffie, for it really did stink in those days. We set off across Ireland, often on single-track roads, always stopping on the bridge in Galway to see the rows of salmon piled up waiting to climb into Loch Corrib. Then on to Oughterard and beyond to the lovely Currarevagh, the beautiful guest house of the Hodgson family, looking out over Loch Corrib.

Who could forget the breakfasts? Porridge with your very own individual pot of cream, then eggs and bacon, the works, all before setting off to fish for sea trout and the odd salmon at Fermoyle. Occasionally we had a day on Corrib, trying to catch the brown trout by dapping* and dry fly†, or by trolling some lure to catch the really big ones, or even possibly a salmon. Currarevagh had boats in a beautiful old boat shed. You could take one out whenever you wanted and paddle about in the glorious bay below the house. In the long summer afternoons, which were too hot for fishing, we played croquet on the lawn and sought out the exotic butterflies.

Fermoyle was then a sea-trout fishery of the highest quality. I pray it has survived the sea-lice ravages of the fish farms that have sprung up since. There was a series of small but prolific connected loughs, a tiny river between each, which meandered slowly down to

---

* Allowing just the fly to touch the surface of the water, off a short line with no casting.

† Where the fly floats on the surface rather than sinking beneath.

the sea. The names were beautiful – Clogher, Shanawonna, Carrick, Dereen – and all the loughs were full of sea trout and the occasional salmon, which were more easily caught in the rivers. A sea trout of four pounds was a big one, but there were masses, weighing between one and four pounds, all caught on little trout rods and the best to eat.

We fished from a boat, drifting, with ghillies at the oars, invariably and inevitably called Pat. They knew their fishing and their loughs. We used mainly wet fly, Blue, Black or Red Pennels, not much else, these being the weapons of choice. They were incredibly effective and we caught so many sea trout, always over a hundred in six or seven days' fishing, that we never kept a proper record. It was just the salmon that we recorded.

My favourite loughs were Clogher and Shanawonna, which could be reached only by walking, a long hike from the car-parking place. There was no boat on Shanawonna, and I caught a salmon there on a breathless, bright sunny day as we fished around the edges. The fish had never seen a fly before.

There was something mysterious and exotic about Fermoyle House. Palm trees in the garden, a reclusive owner we never met. He was a hawker or a falconer and there were strange hawks flying around all the time – or am I imagining that? The last time we went was awkward; unknown to us, after we had booked, the whole place had been sold to the famous O'Brien racing family, who did not really want us there. It was a sad end and we never went back, but it remains a lovely childhood memory. There was something very soft and enchanting about the whole place, and behind the eyes of everyone we met was the twinkle, the charm and the humour.

My only regret was not catching one of those Corrib monster brownies, but then August was not the best time for that. We caught trout up to 3 pounds and a few salmon (I even had one casting off the Currarevagh bay pier with a spinner), and lost something mighty when trolling for those monster trout in the boat, but those 8-pounds-plus heart-stoppers eluded us.

You can still stay there: Currarevagh, just outside Oughterard. It is magic.

My Fishing Book

I started with a small fishing book, which quickly became full, and some kind person, I wish I could remember who, gave me a beautifully bound book from Smythson of Bond Street simply marked FISHING. Some would call it a register, but I am not very keen on that word; it sounds too clinical, so 'book' will have to do. I wonder why I bother to keep it.

Now I am aged seventy-one, my book has maybe just enough pages to 'see me out', if I am lucky enough to live another ten or fifteen years. Perhaps 25 per cent of its roughly 200 pages remain unused – and no, I am not telling you how many fish can fit on a page.

Some keep a book recording every day spent on the river, successful or not. I could not do that because (a) I fish so much and (b) almost never for a full day. Two hours, mostly on summer evenings, is my average, for after that I have both had enough and my neck starts to hurt, a product of RFI, repetitive fishing injury. For the same reason, I never now catch very many in a day; for those days that do have an entry, the number ranges from one to three. Nowhere is there any record of the countless fruitless hours – just as well as it would force me to face up to my incompetence.

The other product of a book covering sixty years is how much my handwriting has changed, not just once but several times. Initially scruffy and all over the place, when I reached twenty-one it became small, incredibly neat and amazingly legible. It has remained small, but is now neither neat nor legible. It seems to have been a gradual process of deterioration, with no obvious watershed moment when it slipped. If I want my writing to be read easily now, I have to print in capitals, or preferably not write longhand at all.

The first entry is for 26 April 1960, a six-pounder in the Weil Stream at Birgham Dub, and the last, at the time of writing, for 3 November 2020 on the Glen, a tributary of the Till, itself a tributary of the Tweed. I caught three old salmon there on my trout rod, 10, 9 and 2 pounds respectively. In between, in the intervening sixty years, is a catalogue of what used to be slaughter, for we killed almost everything, but over the last thirty or so years has been a succession of 'catches and releases', with the odd casualty where the fish swallows the fly and is bleeding too much to be saved. I never deliberately kill salmon now, and have not done so for years.

There are days, even big days, when I was younger and fished for more than two hours, that I had forgotten, but a glimmer of recognition returns when I reread the details. Of the numerous entries with just one salmon caught, unless it was a monster, I have no memory whatsoever.

The purpose of my fishing book remains something of a mystery. I appear to be ruled by that *Mastermind* quizmaster's mantra, 'I've started so I'll finish', without knowing why. When I ask others if they too keep a 'book', so many say they do not but now wish that they had because so many glorious and happy memories have been lost forever. There is a 'remarks' column on the far right of each entry, but I have made that tediously functional and tend to record such minutiae as river heights, the weather and how many other fish were caught that day. For example, the entry for 22 August 2011 says I caught ten on a No. 6 Cascade in four different pools (carefully noted), as were the weights, all between 9 and 13 pounds, with the 'remarks', 'Amazing day, 2ft 3ins and a bit coloured after lots of floods. No grilse. Mostly hen fish and sea-liced, 7 on a full floater and 3 intermediate, all wading.'

The whole book contains just two photographs: one of the immature European Crane that lived on the fields to the east of our house for one whole winter, and the other of my only 30-pounder.

Does any of that get us any further? Does the mounting tally mean very much except that I have fished a lot over the years on the best river in the land? I suppose it is interesting, for example, that I caught four salmon in the worst pool, the Annay, on the day that the record score was made here – sixty-one salmon by four rods on 27 September 2010. 'Remarks' tells me that I rescued my son Richard off the London train to Berwick with an hour of daylight left, and rowed him in the Annay; he caught two more.

Would I have remembered any of that detail without my 'book'? Certainly not. It helps jog the memory of some happy times. That alone is something.

Grandhome

After the Irish Currarevagh summer holiday adventures ended, for another three or four years our parents took us to the River Don in Aberdeenshire, renting the fishing and a little cottage at Grandhome, next to the big house. Although there were salmon about, coming from the Tweed, the real added attraction was the trout fishing. The Don was then – and maybe it still is now – the Test of the north.

We went for two weeks in August, not the easiest month to catch brown trout, but catch them we did, all on a dry fly, and in considerable numbers. Each time we went we caught well over a hundred, averaging amazingly over a pound. There would be a rise in numbers around midday, then our success would be sporadic during the afternoons, depending on the weather. The evenings could be spectacular with trout everywhere, when the fly of choice was a Coachman as it became darker. Otherwise Olives, Greenwells and March Browns did the business during the day. In the three or four years we went, I caught two trout over 4 pounds, and another of just under 4 pounds, rising in the short stream below the cauld,* which I pursued relentlessly until it made a mistake. Another 2-pounder was won only after casting to its left, it having refused a more direct approach. On netting, I found it was blind in its right eye. Another broke my nylon after too strong a strike; after retying an identical fly, I caught the same fish and retrieved the first fly from its mouth.

The few trout we ate had a distinctly bacon-y flavour, Grandhome being just downstream from the outflow of the

---

* Scottish word for dam or weir.

Lawson's bacon factory at Dyce. The last time we went, the efflu-ent had been cleaned up, and the trout were both smaller and no longer tasted of bacon. We knew the pollution was bad, but it was difficult not to look back on those bacon-fed trout with a little guilty nostalgia.

Grandhome was, and I hope still is, owned by the Paton family. In the late 1960s, I remember having tea with my parents and old (or so he seemed) Mr Paton, and seeing their wonderful library.

By the end of the 1960s, we three boys were fleeing the nest, and family summer holidays were over. Younger brother Mark has been back to Currarevagh recently, and found it largely unchanged, still with the wonderful Hodgson family in charge, but I have never been back there, or to Grandhome.

If only for a few hours, I wish I could go back in time, with my family as we then were, to find myself in a boat on Clogher, the wind blowing and the sea trout taking, or stalking one of those monster wild brown trout on the Don as it sips down every fly that comes its way. In my mind, I still can go back. That will have to do.

Eton? I Loved Every Minute

The press likes nothing more than pointing out that so-and-so went to Eton, preferably when he has done something unspeakable; it seems the world's gossipers and trolls cannot get enough. Both my children were there. One spends his life pretending he never was, while the other used to shout it from the rooftops and talk about 'School' as if it is the only one. The trouble is that a lot of us really think that. Call it arrogance, an unbridled sense of superiority, or whatever else. It is a great school. I can only try to explain why I loved it and sent my children there. I suspect what follows will fail to achieve that aim.

I arrived there in 1963, entering Bud Hill's house (BJWH) at South Lawn. We soon moved to a much better, more central and newer House at Baldwin's Bec. There were interestingly named other boys there: Gladstone, Astor, Baring, Montagu-Douglas-Scott, the Master of Forbes, Waterhouse, and many others, and of course there was my older brother. This was at a time when our uncle was prime minister. We had called in at Downing Street for tea before proceeding to Eton.

'Not good,' you are thinking. 'If anyone is going to grow up spoiled and with an insufferable sense of entitlement, that is precisely the way to go about it.'

Hold on; it was not all endless luxury. The younger boys all spent some time as 'fags', running errands for the more senior boys, cooking their tea and so on. Some 'fag masters' could be strict, bordering on the unpleasant, but most were polite, courteous and fair in their dealings, as were mine: Gladstone, Astor and Forbes.

There you are, living with fifty boys in your House for five years, with your own room, a boys' maid (invariably Spanish) to clean the room for you, and a housemaster and his wife (ours was called 'Screech' for obvious reasons). You ate in the House in a communal dining room, except for tea, which was in your rooms. You 'messed' – had tea with – two or three friends from your own year, in my case Dundas and Havelock Allan. One was a scholar and became a serially successful city type and businessman, while the other became a barrister and judge. Good and everlasting friends, I see them both still, even if we live at opposite ends of the country and, annoyingly, they have been more successful than me.

You wear 'school dress', a morning coat and tails, all day, except when playing games, and the regular changing in and out of 'tails' was a daily chore. Too cold in the winter and unbearably hot in the summer – but, I suppose, character-building. In the 1960s we went to either Lower or College Chapel twice a day on weekdays for short services.

Academically I was, still am, middling, but the teaching was spectacular. My tutor, Michael Kidson, was a great man, wholly unconventional in his methods, a true eccentric, and we all looked forward to his lessons and tutorials. We never knew quite what would happen next, but it was both benign and educational. There was a sense of freedom, of being able to decide your own destiny there without pressure. I found university life, what little I had of it, remarkably, and therefore disappointingly, like Eton.

None of which quite explains why we all are as we are. Arrogant? Yes, a bit, but the majority, the good ones, not excessively so. Confident? Yes, but again not overtly so. Treat everyone the same and no respecters of persons? You bet, when you spend five years with a load of toffs, maharajas, sons of billionaires and mega-plutocrats, and both major and minor European royalty, you quickly learn to spot the good from the bad and to deal with them accordingly, no matter how very grand they think they are. We treat everyone on merit. That ridiculous question 'Do you know who I am?' cuts no ice with us; we don't care. You are who you are, good and bad, and no labels, let alone money, will change that.

To be educated at Eton is to have drawn one of life's aces. I have never regretted it for one minute. It is divisive, as all fee-paying private schools are, and I wish every young boy and girl could have the start in life that I had, for that would be fair and just. Absent that, the price is that we lucky ones have to do more; we have to contribute, we have to stand up and be counted and put our luck to good use, certainly not just for our own selfish ends. We are in debt to society, and must repay the debt, big time. It is the only justification.

Have I passed that test in my life, of contributing to society in line with my privileged education and upbringing? If I have, does it justify the huge leg-up, which so many millions never had? There is only one Person who can answer that.

In the meantime, I remain a member of a club, 'the biggest club in the world' as another OE, the cricket commentator Brian Johnston used to call it. Can you spot an Old Etonian at a hundred paces just by how he looks, by his demeanour, by his slight touch of arrogance, of knowing his place in the world, even if he is not standing at the bar in White's, in the Long Room at Lord's, or playing golf at Royal St George's or Swinley? I rather think you can, and, God help me, I usually find, even when I have never met them before, that we have an immediate and invisible bond, the amity of shared experiences. I like them and they are genuine and good people.

For the most part.

'Come out. You have caught enough.'

Few will experience a day's fishing when you can catch as many salmon as you like. Over time, tolerance for numbers has reduced. The other side of the coin is that you carry on and catch as many as possible, payback for those endless days, months and years when nothing was happening. However, when you are a guest, you can catch only as many as you are allowed.

My godfather, Major Jack Briggs, owned the Lees beat on the Tweed jointly with his brother Scott. There was an A-listed mansion house, stables, walled garden, a lodge and more, but they had bought it for the fishing. It cost £12,000 in 1946 (I have the lawyer's original account settlement papers). Scott and Jack already had their houses nearby.

Scott was a racehorse owner, one of which, Macmoffat, came second twice in the Grand National. Scott's Land Rover always had a loaded 12-bore shotgun in the rack, ready to use. He would point it out of the car window and extinguish the life of any unlucky game bird or vermin that he could see over the hedge or roadside fence. It mattered little whose land he was shooting over.

Jack was a gentle person, less frightening than Scott, who could bark, and did, at the younger version of yours truly. Jack was a fine cricketer and deadly at shooting, especially high pheasants. He drew an outline of a seated cat at the bottom of his letters and cards, Pink Panther-like.

They never let the fishing and had one permanent boatman cum ghillie, Taylor, a fearsome big man reputed to have shot a poacher when working at Lennel. History does not relate if the poacher survived or was winged. Occasionally, there was a second boatman called Muckle. There were two fishers at most on two miles of water, more often one. With the exception of the top two pools, the rest was largely unfished, no doubt to the joy and benefit of those opposite.

The first few months of 1960 had been wet, with weeks of floods from Christmas until early February. Fishing began on 8 February and the river was full of spring salmon. Among the ninety-five caught that month, my Uncle Henry had done best, catching eighteen on 22 February. He was the only one fishing on two miles of river and they were all caught in one pool, the Temple. After yet another week of floods, the action began again on Saturday 5 March with fourteen caught, then nineteen on Monday the 7th.

My cousin, Caroline Douglas-Home, had been asked to fish on Tuesday. Jack tried too. They caught thirty-one, all in the Temple, Caroline catching twenty in the top half and Jack eleven in the bottom half of the pool. The comments from Jack's book read, 'Height 2'8", our record and her record. She started at 10 a.m. and landed the 20th at 4.30. Top half of the Temple only, also caught 2 kelts.* I fished Dam to Slap and caught 11, lost 2, sent the fish away (to be sold) and stopped early.' In summary, with an hour for lunch, two of them had caught thirty-one salmon in barely five hours' fishing and in one pool.

Caroline remembers, 'I had caught twenty by 4.30 and was keen to go on but Jack stopped me saying, "Come out. You have caught enough. There will be none left for Hugh tomorrow."' Caroline's record for the Lees lasted one day.

'Hugh' was Major Hugh Cairns, sportsman extraordinaire. The only person fishing the next day and again just in the Temple Pool,

---

* Spawned salmon dropping back to the sea.

he caught twenty-one, lost a few more and broke his rod, wasting valuable fishing time. It was a bitter day with an east southeast wind and snow showers. Hugh told me later that Taylor tied the boat to a tree and Hugh hurled his golden sprat as far as possible. He hooked something almost every cast and said he would have caught many more but for the broken rod and fishing with golden sprats, the sprats having to be 'reloaded' after every fish capture. Guests fishing the next day caught twenty-two and twenty-one the day after that.

Exceptional, no doubt, but that is a flavour of Tweed spring fishing for you in the 1960s. The assumption is that all those fish would have been killed and sold; almost all, after 14 February, were caught spinning.* The routine was to fish with a fly before 14 February, because you had to by law, but from then until the weather warmed up in April, to use a spinning rod, switching to fly and greased line when the water temperature exceeded 45°F.

Jack and Scott died in the 1970s and would be horrified, no doubt, that we now have four rods all year round, and most of the fishing is let. It is illegal to sell rod-caught salmon, and for much of the year you are not allowed to kill them.

They would recognise very little of today's world.

---

* A technique using a spinning lure, usually metal or weighted, to attract fish.

Not Strictly Legal?

I learned as a child what most salmon fishers never will: that the most important part of any river is its faraway upper reaches, not the Junction Pool or whatever other grand beat they are fishing. The future is there, the calm clear water of the Tweed's myriad spawning streams, at its most exquisite after a sharp frost.

The winter holidays from school were my least favourite. No fishing. Christmas Day was at Carham for a superb lunch with my mother's brother and sister-in-law, Billy and Eila Straker-Smith. Then there was shooting, good fun but it never grabbed me in quite the way fishing did. So what could you do during the winter holidays of the 1960s: with no Sky, laptops, DVDs, CDs, iPhones or day-long TV?

My two brothers and I had to amuse ourselves, sometimes roaming around the farm with a gun, trying to find a cock pheasant, a snipe or a woodcock to shoot, decoying pigeons into an old stubble field, or evening duck flighting as they come into land on the pond. Often with my father, a wonderful tutor – it would be he who shot most of the bag.

Running along the northeast boundary of our Easter Langlee farm was the Ellwyn Burn, not big enough to hold salmon for most of the year, but they would come in numbers to spawn. I cannot recall what year in the mid-1960s, but it was very cold and the Ellwyn was low and clear, and full of spawning fish.

I would walk from our house to where the Ellwyn meets the Tweed at Upper Pavilion, and then walk upstream from there, crucially coming up behind any salmon or sea trout before they would see me. For most of the way it was a deep-sided wooded glen but breaking into open countryside the higher it climbed and the closer to the neighbouring Glendearg farm. The pools were small but deep, and in the shallower riffles there would be salmon spawning on the gravel.

The tactic was to approach slowly and with stealth from below, standing still and watching for any underwater movement that would betray a fish. It could be the gentlest wag of a tail, or some dark shape lying in the depths. The plan was to disturb them slightly, enough for them to seek sanctuary under the bank or, a favourite, stick their heads under a part-submerged old tree root. They lacked spatial awareness, incapable of judging that although their head might be hidden under the root, their tail would be wagging in the current, in full view of miscreants and ne'er-do-wells, such as yours truly.

What I did next was illegal, and any bailiff worth his salt would have taken me by the ear, tweaked it viciously and warned me never, ever to do that again. I would roll up my sleeves, lying flat on the bank, leaning out over the edge, right arm into the freezing water. Then I would carefully manoeuvre my hand upstream until it was level with, or fractionally behind, the still-wagging tail, the head nowhere to be seen under the root. I would grab the tail and lift the fish out in one lightning movement.

That was it. A quick look to see if it had spawned, a rough guess at its size and then straight back in the water, before it realised what had happened. Maybe because they were so cold or suffering from temporary shock, they would swim away calmly, often ending up with the tail sticking out from under the same tree root. What fun. I never imagined I was doing anything wrong. Now I am sure I was. Sheriff Patterson, keen angler and scourge of poachers, whom he hated with intense passion, would have disapproved had my case ever come before him.

On the way home, I would cut across the fields and along what was no more than a large ditch that ran into the Ellwyn. In that gravelly ditch would be spawning brown and sea trout. No need to lift them out; they had nowhere to hide. I could usually spot them long before they saw me, and then skirt around them so as not to disturb.

Salmon anglers display a lamentable lack of interest in anything other than whether there are any fish in the river in the week they are there, much as most supermarket shoppers give little thought to the history of their food arriving on the shelf. I learned then that there is nothing so important as those spawning streams to the health of the Tweed. Look after the spawning beds, allow as many salmon as possible to get there, and the fish will do the rest.

Of course it is not that simple – the little remaining river netting, sea lice and disease from west-coast fish farms, drought, flood and predation – there are still many concerns for our rivers and their salmon. But the one thing that is wholly within our control is our spawning areas. As the climate continues to warm, further massive tree planting in the headwaters will be needed to keep water temperatures cool and shaded. That is the biggest challenge. If we manage to meet it, the Ellwyn Burn and its fellow tributaries will continue to provide the production line for future generations of the Tweed's fry, parr and smolts* in decades to come.

Nothing in the salmon world is more important. I am lucky to have witnessed it, first hand, early in my life, in the little Ellwyn Burn.

---

* Fry are recently hatched or juvenile fish; smolts are salmon of one or two years, ready to go out to sea; parr is the stage between the two.

What's in a Name?

Living in Scotland, too far away to be taken out from Eton for the day, it was a joy to be invited to a friend's home, for some normal life, if only for a few hours. Mark's mother and stepfather were incredibly glamorous to a young waif and stray from the far north. I will never forget how kind they were, even if others, those who never met them, may remember them differently. I always think of being there in summer, the walled garden and the swimming pool, and potting a few rabbits after dinner in the park.

I was staying at the home of one of my best friends from school. It was the day of a general election in the 1960s. Mark lived with his stepfather and mother in a glorious house, the Dower House, near Buntingford in Hertfordshire. His mother was Valerie Hobson, that most beautiful and stunning of actresses, *The King and I*, *Kind Hearts and Coronets* and *Great Expectations* among her triumphs on stage and screen.

Valerie had married Anthony Havelock-Allan, David Lean's film producer for such epics as *Great Expectations*, *Oliver Twist* and *Ryan's Daughter*, in 1939. They divorced in 1952, not, I have always thought, because they did not love each other, but because, in the film world, they were so often apart, at the other ends of the world.

In July 1966, Mark and I were fishing a little Cumbrian sea trout river with his father, Anthony. It was the day of England's World Cup triumph, which we watched on the pub's TV. That evening, as we were fishing until dark for sea trout, Anthony complained of not feeling well, despite which he drove us back to the pub. Mark rang his mother who, although long divorced from Anthony, arrived at dawn the next morning, having driven through the night. She shipped him off to the nearest hospital, having correctly diagnosed a heart attack. After lengthy recuperation, he fully recovered. He was only sixty-two at the time and there is no doubt she saved his life. He died thirty-six years later, at the age of ninety-eight.

Back to the Dower House on election night. Luxuriously ensconced and loving the whole experience of staying there, fussed over by Valerie, with Johnny Mathis playing in the background, it was heaven. Always in attendance was the butler, Mr Briscow, nicknamed 'Busty'. Valerie's King Charles spaniel hated him with unbridled loathing. It barked whenever he appeared, and if Valerie wasn't looking, Busty barked back!

Then there was Jack, Jack Profumo, whom Valerie had married in 1954. He was the best and funniest of hosts. Incredibly quick-witted, he made me laugh nearly all the time. He loved what he called the 'folderols', and a small TV was placed in the middle of the dining-room table so as not to miss a moment of variety shows such as *Sunday Night at the London Palladium*. It was a happy house and I loved staying there.

I cannot recall being any too aware of the oddness of sitting watching the election results, late into the night, with Jack, who had caused the biggest political scandal of the twentieth century just a few years earlier, a scandal that had been a factor in bringing down a Conservative government and, quite possibly, shortened my Uncle Alec's term as prime minister. Almost sixty years later, it still fascinates, with the news media appearing unable to move on – but why?

It is the name: Profumo. There was, and is, something exotic about it, mysterious, Italian but more than that: it smells of intrigue, not quite mafia but nearly, and with a particularly aristocratic and

American twist; Cliveden, the Astors, a Russian spy and some call girls; not James Bond but almost.

Would any of this have stuck for so long if Jack's surname had been 'Smith'? I doubt it, 'The Smith Affair' being eminently forgettable where 'The Profumo Affair' is not.

Unlike most others, I never think of Jack or Valerie in that connection. They were unfailingly generous and kind to me over many years, and I will never forget that, or them. Jack and Mark asked me to be an usher at Valerie's funeral service, and I have never been more proud. David – Jack and Valerie's son – writes learned, beautifully written and entertaining articles and books on his favourite subject and passion, fishing. He lives in Scotland, in order to be close to more fish. He wears his name with pride.

As he should.

Camasunary, Skye

When we went to Camasunary first in the late 1950s, it was a two-day journey. With single-track roads with passing places, at least three ferry trips, the first where the Forth road bridges now are at Queensferry, and an overnight hotel stop short of Skye itself, it was a marathon for three 'are we there yet?' young boys. Even on Skye itself, on the second day, it was not straightforward.

Hardy, fit souls could walk over the hill, but we drove to Elgol and into a boat to chug our way around the headland with all the kit and food for a week's stay. I can see it now, the first sight of Camasunary House, whitewashed with the huge bay and sea in front and the almost vertical Cuillin mountains, the highest Blaven, behind, our home in the middle of nowhere. As the little boat drove onto the beach and we all piled out and up the hundred yards or so to the house, it was the ultimate adventure. There was no electricity and the loo was outside, with those friendly midges for company when you were at your most vulnerable.

Our parents were friends of Stevie and Brenda Johnson whose family owned Camasunary, indeed the whole of the Strathaird Estate on the Isle of Skye. As ever, we went for the fishing; the sea trout numbers, and sizes, in the 1950s and 1960s, as with so many other places in the west of Scotland at that time, were spectacular. On that first trip, I was too young to fish other than by lobbing a parentally guided worm into the pools near the sea of the Camasunary river, or into the little trout stream at the north-eastern end of the bay. But even then, the whole place, the adventure, left an indelible mark, despite playing on the beach being more of an attraction than the fishing. That would change.

Stevie was a vet by profession, a keen salmon and sea-trout fisher, and used to take some autumn fishing on my father's Upper Pavilion on the Tweed. Small of stature, he was the most good-natured of people, except occasionally when things were not going his way. His temper was legendarily quick and fiery but, like any flash fire, over in a trice. After losing several salmon, one after the other, at Upper Pavilion, I found him lying on his back on the bank, furiously kicking his feet in the air with an indescribably febrile flow of unrepeatable language. Seconds later he was all smiles and 'hail fellow, well met'.

At a loose end, and without any brothers, I went there again with just the Johnsons and my parents, in my late teens and there-fore old enough to do the fishing some justice. Much time was spent in the sea, the river being low and thereby forbidding the sea trout any means of entry into the river and the ensuing lochs of Na Creitheach and An Athain. The sea was full of them as I waded endlessly in the surf, but success was frustratingly limited. In similar conditions, on another occasion, my father hooked and beached a 10-pound sea trout after an epic battle on his little trout rod. The problem with hooking something large, on light tackle, in the sea is that there is no limit to where the fish can run; he said he could see no reason why his monster should not head for Rhum, Eigg or Muck, then America. He won eventually, but it was a close-run thing.

Stevie, my father and I went out in a boat on Loch Na Creitheach, a short walk behind the house, in the evenings. We took it in turns to row and fish, the rower in the middle with a fisher at each end. It was a long-standing tradition in the Johnson family that if you caught a sea trout of 8 pounds or more, you had to make a life-size paper outline and drawing of it, to put on the house walls. I caught my 8-pounder in the bay on the right-hand side of the loch, directly opposite Moony Point, so called because that is where most of the big sea trout are caught and, for reasons I cannot remember, they are called 'Moonies'. You will not find my Moony on the walls, as I cannot draw and was reluctant to expose my inadequacies to the ridicule of posterity. Sometimes the outboard motor would take us to the top end of Na Creitheach; from there it was a short walk to the much smaller top loch An Athain. We never did much good there, the fish being that much longer in the tooth and less likely to take a fly.

Of the three amazing sea-trout lochs, by far the most spectacular was Coruisk. You could walk there, over something called 'the big step', which sounded, and was, sufficiently frightening that I always went round to Coruisk, another river system entirely, by sea and boat. The entrance to Coruisk river was stunning, seals, cormorants and otters everywhere, and you could fish the river before going on up the short distance to the glorious, incredibly clear-watered loch. Stevie's temper operated on an especially short fuse at the sight of all those fat seals, each one of which he imagined, probably correctly, had become fat on the sea trout he had been hoping to catch in Coruisk. Because we were too many to go in the smaller loch boat, I was deposited, as the youngest and fittest, with rod in hand, on a tiny but beautiful island in the middle of Coruisk. To this day, I can see those huge sea trout, so clear was the water, swimming in dark shadows below me, as I fished round the circumference of the island. I caught nothing and could not understand why all those cruising monsters had ignored my flies. Annoyingly, the boat fishers had done very much better. The most dramatic and beautiful of mountains surrounding you will take your breath away, even if, like me, you catch no fish.

The last time I went was when Stevie invited Jane and me shortly after we were married. I knew it was high risk, a long shot. The midges in the loo were the final straw; Jane pretty much said that if I wanted to holiday there again, I was on my own. She generally likes to be within easy reach of Tesco, and have electricity and the comforts of home on tap. Camasunary can offer many delights, but the requirements that Jane considers essential are not among them.

By then, most of the Strathaird Estate, excluding Camasunary and the fishing, had been sold to Ian Anderson of Jethro Tull's popular-music fame. One teatime, I was tucking into some cake when Stevie's hackles visibly rose as he heard a noise and spotted some smoke coming over the hill track. By then you could come over the hill in a 4x4, as opposed to walking or going round by sea. As the noise and smoke, plus mounted and helmeted motorbike rider, came closer and closer, into Stevie's domain, his legendary temper went into full attack mode. The bike stopped, as did the noise and exhaust smoke, just outside the house. Stevie's face by now was bright red, and all that was needed was ignition. As the biker's helmet was removed, the transformation in Stevie was both astonishingly rapid and complete as he beamed at his visitor. It was Ian Anderson, come to pay a neighbourly visit, and to try out his new toy on the hillside terrain.

After Stevie and his brothers died, Camasunary was taken on by his nephew Alan, who loves it and looks after it with care and devotion. The fishing is a shadow of its former self and may never again be as I remember it. There are seals everywhere, which cannot help, but the collapse, as with Loch Maree and so many other locations on the Scottish west coast, was suspiciously coincidental with the arrival of salmon fish farms, with all their well-known escapees, disease, sea lice and other issues. I fear the sea trout will never proliferate as they once did, or at least not until those fish farms are removed from the marine environment. Camasunary's sea trout are yet another example of man's ability to wreck something unique and natural, even in the most remote of places.

Before signing off, I googled Camasunary, and to my relief the pictures look exactly as it did over sixty years ago, standing proudly whitewashed in that wonderful bay looking out over the sea to Rum, Eigg and Muck, with Blaven towering overhead. At least some things never change.

A Breed Apart

There is a largely invisible, if certainly not silent, army out there, on the river. Further north they would be called 'ghillies' and the name is creeping southward, but on the Tweed they are known as 'boatmen'. When the water is high, they spend their time rowing boats for their visiting anglers. You can argue that the larger share of the salmon caught this way is because of the boatman's skill, something my friends learn very quickly when I am rowing them. Here is a flavour of this unseen army of men, for men they mainly are (so far).

They are skilled both in the science of maximising the chances of their anglers catching fish but also in the art, for such it is, of handling a boat. This is often in the most testing of conditions: on a big river, in stormy weather and with a considerable load – the angler – aboard, acting like an unruly mast in the wind.

There is something about the job that breeds character, a fiercely independent spirit and mind; they are opinionated, excellent company. Theirs might seem an easy job when the fish are taking, but customer satisfaction is not so readily come by on those long days when the fish will not take or, worse still, when they are not even there to be caught. It is then that the boatmen's fund of tales will come in useful to regale and encourage the jaded and disappointed angler who has turned his back on his office and is longing for some action.

With so many characters, stories abound. At the Birgham Dub on a good spring fishing day in the 1960s, the fish were taking and, rowing midstream, the boatman looked over towards the bank and saw a body, a corpse, going around and around in an eddy between the boat and the bank. The angler became flustered, suggesting they stop fishing and call the authorities. The boatman demurred. 'You are doing just fine as you are, sir. There is nothing we can do for that poor soul and you are catching fish. He will still be there at lunchtime. We can do all the right things by him then.' Clearly a man who had his sporting priorities right.

Mr Swan, the old Carham boatman during those amazing spring years from the 1930s to the 1950s, whenever his rod suggested going down a notch in size of fly, would gently say, 'I wouldn't do that if I were you, sir. There's no point in testing their eyesight.'

The long-time Lees boatman, Mr Taylor, or 'Taylor' to my godfather Jack Briggs but never to me, was a big man, not to be trifled with, and I spent many an hour talking to him in his retirement, reliving all the stories and big fishing days here during the 1950s and the 1960s, and at Lennel, where he was before coming here. In general, he had, with a few notable exceptions, a very poor opinion of anglers.

One rod — I rather think he was a vicar — had, despite his incompetence, hooked something large. Mr Taylor noticed that the great fish had run three times to exactly the same place up the river, not far from the bank. In his view, they would never land it as the good vicar was being far too weak. So, after half an hour or more, he waded in and positioned himself with his net in the same spot, seventy yards upstream and near the bank. The mighty fish did exactly the same thing for a fourth time and swam straight into Mr Taylor's waiting net. It weighed over 40 pounds and all the boatman would say was, 'If I hadn't done that, we would either have been there still, or it would have got off', giving not an ounce of credit to the poor vicar who had actually caught it.

Jim Mitchell, head boatman on the Birgham Dub, was row-ing my old friend Christopher Wills late one August morning. Christopher was landing a few, but having far too many pulls and losses for Jim's liking. He was already in a peevish mood by lunch-time because of Christopher's carelessness, and when he rowed James Euston in the afternoon exactly the same thing happened, far too many pulls and losses. Having bitten his tongue, he finally snapped and barked, 'You'll no be related to Mr Wills, are you, Lord Euston?'

Unlike their colleagues on other rivers, our boatmen really row the boat. It is hard work and it can be dangerous. On the Tay, they have outboard motors and anchors; on the Spey there are anchors and long ropes, and on the Dee, in common with most other smaller Scottish rivers, they hardly use boats at all. Not only do our boatmen row the boat, but they can rope it from the bank, a skill all of its own, and row the boat with a dragging anchor, much needed with a big wind and heavy, running water.

Some used to work on the nets. Others have been keen fish-ermen in the past and not necessarily always on the right side of the law. Their experience has proven a huge benefit later, as they know the water best and from a long time back. Now the stoutest defenders of the status quo, proud possessors of that much heralded 'poacher turned gamekeeper' trait, they know where the bodies are buried – metaphorically speaking, of course.

Many fewer salmon would be caught without our boatmen. By no means always but too often we anglers claim our own triumphs as just that, our own. 'I caught six today at Sprouston', or at the Junction, Floors, Wark, Mertoun or wherever else. No doubt you did, but did you really, or was it just as much the man in the boat, sitting, perhaps not so quietly, behind you?

They are a special breed. Our Tweed boatmen.

'You had better come over here, boy!'

One of the most wonderful places to fish on the Tweed is Middle Mertoun: double bank, glorious streams, totally secluded, no roads and in the most beautiful part of the Borders. That my godfather owned it and occasionally asked his godson to fish was just a tad fortunate. My fishing book tells me that I first went there as an eleven-year-old lad on 26 April 1962 and caught three salmon on a greased line and Hairy Mary double.* The boatman tried the north side of the House stream from the boat, then moved us over to the south side and I fished it off the bank. I caught those three salmon one after the other, 10, 9 and 9 pounds of stunning Tweed springers, in exactly the same place; I never moved. Middle Mertoun has been synonymous with magic to me ever since, as the following tale will confirm.

My parents chose three wonderful godparents for me: my aunt (Lady) Bridget Douglas-Home (aka 'Glitterknickers'), Major J. M. (Jack) Briggs MC, and John (aka 'Stinker John'), the Earl of Ellesmere, later Duke of Sutherland. I mention this all at once, you see, to avoid drip-fed name-dropping.

The origins of the nicknames escape me, for I have no idea if Lady Bridget's knickers really did glitter; it seems unlikely. She always dropped her final 'g's as in 'How are you gettin' on?' or 'How are you doin'?' John was certainly no stinker; he was a most unassuming and self-effacing man, rather un-ducal and with a permanent mischievous twinkle in his eye. He called my younger brother Mark 'Nellie'.

---

* A hairwing fly particularly good for salmon.

My father and John were stalwarts of that august body, the River Tweed Commissioners, always sitting together in the front row at meetings (there are eighty-one Commissioners), never contributing at all to the proceedings, but always commenting sotto voce on those who did. 'Who is that dreadful fellow?' or 'We don't really like him, do we?' accompanied by barely, but just audible, giggles, like two naughty schoolboys in class. I first witnessed this when I too joined that revered body in my early thirties when they were in their sixties. They never ceased to amuse each other. One a guest of the Germans and held in Colditz, the other detained by the Japanese in prison camps in Burma, they deserved their fun.

John and Jack were my father's best friends, enjoying regular evening phone calls to discuss the next sporting adventure, some past slaughter, the state of the river, or in Jack's case all of the above plus cricket. And with both, always the weather. Jack and his brother Scott owned the Lees beat of the Tweed, where I now live.

On the morning of 3 October 1969 I was waiting to 'go up' to Oxford, when the phone rang just after breakfast. It was John.

'Are you doing anything today?'

'No,' I replied expectantly.

'Well then, you had better come over here, boy!'

A previous guest had called off. 'Here' was Middle Mertoun and I was to have it all to myself for the day, plus Mr Brown the ghillie.

I arrived around 11 a.m. The river was beery, but fining down after a flood. I cannot remember Mr Brown looking at all optimistic, and after starting at the top, in the Webbs, not seeing much and without a pull after half an hour or so, nor was I. I dropped down to the next pool, the Craig (full name 'Craigo'er') with the same sinking line and medium-sized black-and-yellow tube fly.

What happened next, in sixty years of salmon fishing, I have never known before, or since.

I went down the Craig twice, and from the start salmon were showing everywhere. The first time I had well over twenty 'offers'; we lost count. I landed just four of them. The second time, on Mr Brown's advice changing to a bigger fly and bigger hooks as they were clearly 'taking short', I had another eleven 'offers' and landed six of them. In under three hours (lunch was late that day) I had had around forty offers in one pool and landed ten of them, all beautiful silver salmon and half of them over 15 pounds, biggest 23 pounds. I was surprised if the fly ever completed its journey round without being pulled.

To have landed proportionately so few might seem incompetent, but through it all there were constant debriefs with Mr Brown, standing by my side. We tried everything, pulling it round faster, not pulling it round at all, giving some slack when they took, and not giving any slack at all, if anything even pulling back. Nothing seemed to work.

In the short time left after lunch and before finishing at 5 p.m., I caught two more in the wonderful pools below the Craig, the only two more pulls I had. In a short day, I had caught twelve stunning salmon.

So what had happened? There was nothing to be seen or caught when I started in the Webbs, and no great numbers afterwards in the pools below the Craig. The only conclusion is that my arrival in the Craig at around 11.30 a.m. had coincided with a huge shoal of salmon settling into the pool, having moved upstream in the flood the previous day and overnight. That would explain the poor taking, typical of salmon that have just appeared but have not yet settled into their lies, resting in the calmer water after their exertions in the rapids between pools.

Most of those caught went back, which was an unusual practice at the time, but I did not want any and some of the bigger ones were left with Mr Brown for my godfather to have smoked. I remember worrying that I had caught too many, but a phone call that evening from John ('Well done, boy') put my mind at rest.

It was, by any salmon-fishing standards, an extraordinary, once-in-a-lifetime event, with over forty salmon hooked in so short a time. I, and no doubt many others, have caught and landed more salmon in a full day of fishing, but few will ever experience anything like it.

SUMMER

S ummer – June right through to the end of August – is a time to which most of us look forward. Yet in the salmon-fishing world it has not always been so. Not long ago, very few Tweed anglers bothered to fish for salmon in the summer, so efficient were the nets at extracting them all before they could get past Coldstream. After 2003, with the demise of most drift netting off the Northumbrian coast, that all changed. For a decade after that, Tweed's fishermen averaged 16,000 salmon a year until 2014 when our fabled autumn run collapsed, and it has not recovered up to the time of writing in 2021. Scientists predict that our salmon will now come back earlier, in the spring and summer, and there is good historical precedent for that. It has happened before, between the 1900s and 1920s, and lasting well into the 1960s, with a massively dominant spring run. And yet, the jury is out. The year 2020 tended to confirm the theorists, with a big late spring and summer run, whereas 2021 has been the opposite, with no fish in any numbers appearing until late July. Relying on precedent is problematic, however, as we don't know what impact rising sea temperature, caused by rampant global warming, might now be having on these cycles.

The problem with summer fishing is drought and heat. Everyone, all weather forecasters, rejoice at the Azores high settling in for the summer. Not we Tweed salmon anglers; we need water and the weather not too hot. It is my pick of times, especially in those long, calm and often solitary evenings when it can be light until 10.45 p.m. – just me, the birds, the mesmeric flow of water, the peace of a summer's evening, and perhaps a fish to be caught; my heaven.

Then, in the gloaming, there are big trout to be had on the dry fly, and sea trout aplenty if you have the energy and time to stay up late enough until darkness comes, and of course, just sometimes, some of those big summer salmon after a welcome July/August flood. Far too quickly, the nights draw in and we relight our Aga at the end of August as the autumn chills take hold. The water begins to cool, the fish are safe from the horrors of drought and heatwaves, and summer on the river is over.

Summer ended for me in 1990 at the age of forty, when just about everything went wrong.

After the Oxford debacle, I had become a chartered accountant in London and Edinburgh. Jane and I were married on a peerless day on 17 May 1980. We moved to the smaller version of our present house in the Borders in 1981. Jane gave birth to our three children in the 1980s, and we have been here, after six extensions to that small house, ever since. The accountancy firm I started in Kelso was going well – it now employs seventy-five people, mostly no thanks to me – and we lived in a most beautiful place. It is a story of privilege, luck and idyll.

That was until 1990. My summer ceased abruptly and disastrously that year with the tragic death of our boy, Freddie.

Our Very Own Piece of Heaven

We have lived here at the Lees, just outside Coldstream, on the banks of the Tweed for forty years. The river is a gentle hundred-yard stroll across the garden from my front door. I walk by it every day, either with my dogs or with a rod, or both. Even without the fishing it would be a wonderful place to live, with its massive and wondrous pre-Victorian and Victorian trees (monkey puzzle, Wellingtonias, beech, oak, lime, chestnut and so on), a beautiful, mainly woodland garden, its water frontage and a view to die for over to Wark village and beyond. Sandbanks (thankfully) it ain't, but with the fishing, well, it is heaven for me, and would be for so many others who like to cast a fly in pursuit of the king of fish. Here is a short guided tour of the Lees beat, my family's very own slice of the greatest UK salmon river.

Our house entrance and gates (so grand!) lie well within the Coldstream 30 (now 20) mph limit, yet we have unbroken countryside on two sides, and the river on the third. Curiously, such is its almost circular meander that we look south, west and east over the river into England. Come the deluge, the Tweed could find its way through our house and grounds, straight to Coldstream bridge, and we would lose over two miles of fishing. I am comforted both that it will not happen in my lifetime and that, even if it did, it would be a seismic event of such proportions that losing a bit of river might be the least of our concerns.

That it contains such good fishing is partly a result of the almost 360-degree bend from the top of the Temple Pool to Leet Mouth at the bottom. Completely straight rivers tend to contain fewer pools or the necessary deep water to attract salmon, whereas we have a perfect mixture of deep slow pools and fast shallower ones, mainly on a curve. Whatever the water height, we can do well, and being only fifteen river miles from tidal waters, even in drought conditions the salmon can get here. In high water we are about the first place salmon stop. In short, both the make-up and diversity of our pools, and their distance from the sea, are pretty well ideal. In width, it varies from over 120 yards wide in the Temple Pool to under 50 in Cornhill Bend.

Some 60 per cent of the salmon are caught in the uppermost three pools, Temple Pool (a long flat dub over 500 yards long), the Cauld stream (a fast stream) and Learmouth stream (ditto). The Temple Pool and the Cauld stream owe their existence in current form to a cauld that separates them, with a 30-foot gap (or slap) in the middle. Both the cauld and the Temple Pool's retaining wall were built in the 1850s, as part of the provision of water via a mill race (or lade) behind our house, to power the old Coldstream mill (now defunct). That both cauld and wall are still in such good nick is testament to how well the Victorians built.

Below the Learmouth stream, as you continue around the never-ending bend, are pools Back of the Wall (the wall is now under the pool, not alongside it), the Glide, Cornhill Bend and Duddo Mouth (the Duddo being a stream coming in from the south side). Below that again are Baby House, Middle Stream, Bags and Annay, the last going to our bottom boundary where the Leet, another small tributary, comes in from the northern side.

Except for a half-mile section from the bottom of the Temple Pool to the top of Learmouth stream, we have just the north bank. Thus far I have avoided using the terms Scottish and English. With exception of that half-mile, the south bank is all in England. Quite why that half-mile and the field that the riverbank borders are in

Scotland remains a mystery, despite extensive research. What fun we will have come Scottish independence and the need for border controls. Bad enough the border being the middle of a mighty river; even worse when some of the land on the south side is Scottish not English. Enough of that.

So there we have it, two miles of beautiful water. Bar 300 yards between the Cauld stream and Learmouth stream where it is too shallow, all fishable, and you can pretty much catch salmon in every yard of it. We have five boats to be used when waters are high but, for the most part, although wide, it is all wade-able and good fly water.

It is our little bit of this great river, and our beautiful house and gardens are right there, on its banks. I love it.

Bouldering

There is a unique excitement about arriving somewhere new; so often the reality, especially with fishing, is disappointment. It needs only one of the many variables – too little water, too much, no fish, too hot, they won't take, and on and on – to be in play for the trip to be less than hoped for. We wait for our annual Scottish highland fishing trips with dream-filled anticipation. Just every now and then they exceed expectations, even when predictions are poor. Maybe that is why we carry on going?

I have done nothing similar before or since, nor have I seen anything quite like the Little Gruinard, top left of Scotland as you look at the map. We called it 'bouldering'.

Johnny and Fiona Warrender had taken the fishing and an adjoining lodge for a week. We were there for just short of three days. It was July 1983 and hot, no rain for three weeks past and we were not expecting the fishing to be good. Maybe it is different now, but then you drove to a bridge close to where the river enters the sea, parked and walked upriver, into the hills, along a path with the tumbling, crystal-clear, mainly white water on your left. It was my first sight of the small but dramatic Little Gruinard, anticipation mounting as we walked away from the road.

I wore wellington boots and had an 8-foot trout rod, even though we were after salmon. There were some named pools, but not many. No ghillie, we had the whole river to ourselves. It took us time to catch on. We started fishing the named pools, as you do, with size-10 flies. So narrow, no cast was more than a few yards, nor did you ever have to get in the water. The named pools could be fished in five minutes each.

I rose one, as did my host, and then some more. Luckily, he had some mini-flies, conventional theory being that if they rise but do not touch, you go smaller. By then we had covered most of the named pools and had nothing to show for it, but at least there had been interest.

Liking new territory, comparatively unexplored, less fished and off the beaten track, I set off as far as I could reasonably go in the time, further upriver where few if any of the pools were named, right into the hills, not as far as the feeder loch at the top, but nearly. I stopped at some flat currentless pools, so unlike the rest, and fished my way downriver, into the tumbling boulder-strewn white water below, flicking my size-14 Logie into any ease, any likely-looking spot, especially just in the lee of those huge boulders.

How it worked! I did not know it then, but it was much like dibbling, skimming or hitching,* my tiny fly dancing in the white water, just on or below the surface. I rose, pulled, lost and caught any number of salmon and grilse; the river was full of them, able to get in because of the water in the feeder loch at the top, despite the recent lack of rain.

I caught five in the two and a half days on my little trout rod, weights 7, 7, 6, 5 and 5 pounds. My fishing book says 'at least 10 more rises and pulls, the most exciting fishing, fish behind almost every boulder; all fresh and 6 more caught by others'.

What magic. The polar opposite of my beloved, but huge, Tweed. Almost forty years later the memory lingers. I have never been back and I'm not even sure I want to, for any return could tarnish a perfect memory. I worry that that glorious little river has

---

* Dibbling is making the fly dance on the water. Hitching is using a fly on the surface of the water to create a 'V', imitating a wake and encouraging a fish to attack.

been affected by the blight of sea lice from nearby fish farms. I hope not, for it was a gem.

If you are ever lucky enough to go there, and some fish are in, you will be able to experience what we came to call 'bouldering', for behind every one of those massive rocks, there were fish.

William

We are all complex, even if we pretend to the world at large that we are not. That William happened to be my uncle was the greatest fortune, and because he lived in Hampshire and we in the Borders, we never saw enough of him and his family.

My Uncle William, my father's next eldest brother, the third of the five brothers, was to me, and many others, the most lovable of men, but an enigma. A joke or a quip was never far from his lips, the sillier the better, but I noticed his children never laughed as much at the constant stream of jokes. They had heard them before.

He was also prone to endless practical joking, often with his oldest friend, Brian Johnston ('Johnners'), the cricket commentator. I was told that William was sent down from Oxford, a long-standing tradition in my family, for tying a police-car bumper to a lamp post, and waiting for the inevitable to happen when it drove off . . . without its bumper. His jokes often backfired, for instance when, in order to disrupt the grand ladies' Sunday afternoon stroll along the Leet, the little river that runs behind the family home at The Hirsel, he had pre-placed a plastic crocodile in the water just below the bridge over which the perambulation was bound to go. On arriving there, and to ensure success and a good deal of ladylike gasps and screaming, William pointed the crocodile out to his mother, Lady Home – Lil to her friends – as the party was on the bridge. A Lambton, and therefore eccentric and unflappable by birth, Lady Home took one look at the half-submerged animal and without turning a hair said, 'Good Lord, William, I had no idea they came this far north', and carried on walking.

I adore anyone who makes me laugh. Here is some of his surprising story.

He was a playwright, author of countless successful plays, arguably the most prolific British playwright of the twentieth century with over forty to his name. Often derided by the critics for the large-country-house, aristocratic, drawing-room-type nature of most of his works, he was nevertheless consistently popular with his audiences and had huge box-office hits, often with more than one play on in London's West End at the same time.

He tried several times to become an MP, never succeeding and standing on different platforms at successive elections, prompting brother Alec to ask, 'Who is William standing for this time?' He most volubly supported the Liberals while his elder brother was both prime minister and leader of the Conservative Party. Alec bore no rancour. They were the greatest of friends, always conferring by phone in the evenings about which nag would be the winner of the 2.30 at Plumpton the next day. He had a horse that ran in the Derby.

When trying to impress strangers, I am prone to saying, 'My grandfather [Straker-Smith] played rugby for the New Zealand All Blacks and my uncle was court-martialled in the Second World War' – both equally unlikely, and both true.

Uncle William was court-martialled for disobeying an order in the Allied attack on the German garrison in the French city of Le Havre in 1944. He was the only one of over 3 million British soldiers in the Second World War to be convicted for wilful refusal to obey an order.

One of his best friends, General Sir David Fraser, a great professional soldier, dealt with the whole subject, expertly and in great depth, in his biography of William, entitled just *Will*.

It was the late summer of 1944. The German commander Colonel Wildermuth led 11,000 men in occupation of Le Havre, and was ordered to defend it 'to the last man'. He could never hope to win, but his job was to tie up as many enemy troops as he could in order to hold up the Allied advance into France, and to deny the Allies the use of Le Havre as a port for as long as possible. He knew defeat was inevitable, but was determined to do his duty.

On 4 September, Colonel Wildermuth asked the Allied commander, General Crocker, to agree to a forty-eight-hour truce so that the French civilian population could be evacuated on 5 and 6 September. General Crocker demanded the unconditional surrender of the German forces in Le Havre. Crocker refused to allow the evacuation, as he saw it as a delaying tactic during which the Germans would destroy the port infrastructure. Wildermuth, following orders, refused unconditional surrender.

The consequent inevitable artillery and aerial bombardment came in three waves and resulted in five thousand deaths, mostly French civilians and all killed by Allied bombing. In the first of the three waves, two thousand French civilians were killed and just nineteen German soldiers.

William, on hearing of the German offer to evacuate civilians and that the Allies had turned it down, refused to take any part in the forthcoming assault on Le Havre.

On 4 October 1944 his court-martial took place. He was found guilty and sentenced 'to be cashiered and to suffer one year's imprisonment with hard labour'. On 23 October 1944 he was admitted to Wormwood Scrubs as a prisoner. He was now a civilian. His father, Lord Home, would come and visit him, insisting on calling in on the prison governor before he left to thank him for 'putting up with William'.

I hope David Fraser would not have minded me quoting his final paragraph on the Le Havre assault and on William:

> Will oversimplified. It is improbable (those who knew him well would say impossible) that fear of personal risk played any part in the way he decided to act. His whole conduct from the beginning had been consistent and there is no reason to doubt the sincerity of his attitude, while its courage is beyond question. He was sick at heart about the war and the way it was going. He hated what he thought of as a smug self-congratulation about the virtues of our own side, engaged in a crusade (alongside the Soviet Union, improbable crusaders) and the evils of the enemy. He loathed double standards as he saw them. He abominated cruelty. Suffering and humbug turned knives in his heart. He needed to shout a protest and it was unlikely to be impeccable in logic, or particularly just, or even reasonable. At each twist of the argument there is a rational point to counter. But, in the ultimate, we are left with 5,000 dead, a devastated French city, and a slender, lonely, defiant figure in British uniform proclaiming that there had to be another way, and prepared to face prison for it.

Do I think William was right? Probably not. Yet I cannot ignore the fact that as a result of his actions the French civilians at Calais and Dunkirk were spared the same fate at the hands of Allied bombers.

David Fraser concludes:

> An attempt may be made to strike a balance in William Douglas-Home's character as a playwright and, more importantly, as a man. Nothing of it conveys that most elusive element to trap with words . . . his personality, and nothing

will. Wherever he touched the lives of others he enriched and brought fun to them. Those who knew him only as a friend knew him to be unique. To the huge mass of his acquaintance who mourned him, who had laughed with him, argued with him, furiously attacked his views or wryly supported them, criticised his attitudes, enjoyed or damned his plays, revelled in his hospitality . . . to these, perhaps to all of these, he was probably the sweetest-natured, most amusing and most lovable human being they had ever known.

My most precious and abiding memory is of sitting with him in the garden of his beloved Drayton House in Hampshire on a glorious summer's evening in the 1970s, looking out over the Meon Valley, and watching the comings and goings of a nuthatch to its nest, feeding its young. He was in sparkling form as the jokes flowed.

My Uncle William, an enigma and a wonderful man.

A Cricketing Dilemma

In 1970 I was sent down from Oxford. What to do? A career in cricket or qualify for something else that would earn a crust? I chose the latter, which I will always regret but was, I suppose, the 'sensible' decision.

Throughout my ten-year schooling at Aysgarth and Eton, I was always in the top teams for my year at cricket. An all-rounder at Aysgarth, my batting was horribly exposed at Eton. I was a bowler, not fast, perhaps fast medium, at Oxford where Vic Canning, our coach at Eton, saw me and proclaimed I had 'put on a yard of pace', after knocking over the first few Eton 1st XI batsman on Upper Club, the year after I left Eton, for the Oxford Authentics.

I topped the bowling averages both in my second year in the Eton XI, and in my only year at, and playing for, Oxford. I did not get a Blue, my philosophy tutor, Oscar Wood, advising me that if I did not stop playing cricket he would ask the Christ Church dean to send me down before taking prelims. He did not 'get' my preference for cricket on the Parks over reading Bertrand Russell, which is strange. I stopped playing cricket, took prelims, failed them, and was sent down anyway.

So ended my serious cricketing career – or did it? I had taken the first three Warwickshire wickets before having Dennis Amiss dropped at slip, a sitter, for nought. He went on to make 70 and the great M. J. K. Smith over a hundred. Then there was Lancashire, one of the best teams in the land at the time. I got Harry Pilling and David ('Bumble') Lloyd, two down for little, then another dropped catch before Barry Wood and the even greater Clive Lloyd started making hay. I played other games, but I recall those two quite vividly.

I needed help, and where better than the *Test Match Special* star commentator Brian Johnston and that superlative cricketing scribe for *The Times*, John Woodcock, the Sage of Longparish? I sat in the Lord's commentary box with Brian and John Arlott, and then repaired for some lunch with Brian and John Woodcock. Apart from being enormous fun, the advice was sound: 'Unless you think you can make it in cricket to the very top, i.e. into the England team, don't stay in cricket, there is no money in it.' In other words, do something else. I still had in the back of my mind that, whereas I thought I could, on a good day, get out many or even most county batsman, there was no doubt that I held few fears in the Parks at Oxford for Messrs M. J. K. Smith and Clive Lloyd, England and West Indian captains respectively.

So that was it. I played on and off for the Eton Ramblers, for I Zingari (until my old friend Johnny Becher's father, the president, kicked me out), and for Jim Swanton's Arabs while I stayed in the south, then just a little bit for the Borderers after moving north, but I was never any good again. The problem with bowling, or at least with my bowling, is that I became good only after playing a lot, by getting into a groove. If you play once every other weekend, that never happens. Eventually disillusionment took over, and I gave up before I was thirty.

Sadly, I sometimes look back at my record and wonder. Two games of 7 wickets for almost nothing against two Yorkshire prep-school sides (a friend took a picture of the scores from the Aysgarth notice board), all 10 in a junior House side at Eton, then Paddy Croker, a beak (master) at Eton gave my son Richard, when he was there, a full record of his father's Eton and Oxford stats, which even I (although not son Richard!) thought were surprisingly impressive. Those were some of the highlights, but at the end of it all, and despite Vic Canning saying I had put on a yard of pace, the truth is that I was never quite quick enough to make it to the very top. For that you need a natural gift, proper 'hurry-up' pace, to worry the very best.

I played with some great cricketers who either did, or almost did, make it. Charlie Crowhurst (Cottenham) my first Eton captain was a great, properly quick, fast bowler. Johnny Barclay, the best of men, an off-spinner and batsman at Eton, went on to far, far greater things with Sussex and England. Then there were Victor Cazalet and Mark Faber, both great batters, the latter also making his mark with Sussex. It is a great sadness that Charlie and Mark died far too young.

Compared with them I was a journeyman trundler, 'metronomic' as my old friend Tom Fort once so generously described me. The inevitable fate, perhaps, of all journeymen metronomic trundlers, I became a chartered accountant.

Three in Three

Those who go to Russia will not see the point. Those destined to fish forever in the UK will. Some come here after ten years of catching nothing, hopefully slaying that dragon while here. Had there been an adjudicator, he or she would have confirmed that I really did have just three casts.

Now loads of salmon anglers will have caught two salmon in two casts; you catch one, you go back in and you hook and land another with your first proper cast. But three?

When we first came to live here in the early 1980s, we did not let the fishing properly. There was a family friends' arrangement whereby they paid £1,000 p.a. to fish every day on the whole two miles.

'What?!' I hear you cry.

How much was the Tweed levy at the time? £1,200 p.a. So, yes, we made a loss and they had almost all the fishing. Part of the deal was that my father and his family could fish pretty much whenever we wanted, but normally only at weekends and on bank holidays, or early mornings and late evenings, because we were busy working. It is impossible to imagine now, and it worked well for a few years until we discovered, when I came to live here, that the family friends hardly fished it at all. We would catch many more in our one day a week than they would on the other five.

I digress.

While this arrangement was still in place, on 29 October 1982, I fished the Cauld stream, wading, before going to work. I had three casts and caught three sparkling fresh grilse, 7, 6 and 6 pounds respectively. A quick change of clothes and off to work. It was extraordinary, for me at least. You would not want it to happen too often. How many more would I have caught had I continued all day? Those who annually make the pilgrimage to the Ponanga(?!),* whatever that is, in Russia, may catch ten in ten casts. So what? That ain't the UK.

Our friends, the tenants, caught just two in the rest of the day on the whole two-mile beat. Unsurprisingly, we started letting it commercially the following year, despite our tenant friends announcing that in their view the Lees was not a good enough beat to let.

Ahem!

---

* As I often call the two most famous salmon rivers in Russia, the Ponoi and Yokanga.

A Skimmer at Cambus O'May

On almost every river in the UK now, over 90 per cent of the salmon caught by rod and line are released back into the water. There is nothing wrong with this, quite the opposite, the absolute priority being to allow our scarce salmon to spawn and to keep the species going. We can no longer pretend we are fishing for anything other than sport, certainly not to provide ourselves with food.

It is my firm and unshakeable belief that, in the pursuit of such an iconic and noble quarry, we should fish only with a fly, by far the most skilful and sporting option, and that spinning, if allowed at all, should be confined to conditions (flood and tempest) when it is impossible to use a fly, or to those who cannot physically wield a fly rod. This means being inventive with the sort of lines and flies we put on the end of our rods, in order to provide some variety. I have a cousin who catches salmon by dapping on the River Mallart and I know others who have caught them with a dry fly or 'Bomber'. Here is an example from the glorious River Dee of what, in a very small way, I have done, but it demonstrates the point.

The first time the magically named Cambus O'May on Royal Deeside appears in my fishing book is on 4 June 1982. Clare Carson is the proprietrix. I caught one salmon in Glashan pool on a Hairy Mary, and the comments read, 'Glorious sunshine for three days, masses of fish but water temperature over 70°F. Two others caught in the three days by four rods. Three weeks ago they caught ninety-three on the same beat in the week.' I can still recall looking from the high bank above Clarach, just one of the many lovely pools, and, so clear is the Dee water, being able to see rows and rows of salmon lying there, comatose in the heat.

John and Clare keep a week for themselves in the late spring, and as two of their most unashamedly sponging friends, we have been lucky to be asked. The reciprocal imperative, which normally applies to friends who are so generous, went flying out of the window with John and Clare Carson many years ago. In simple terms, we can never repay their multitude of kindnesses over so many years. The glorious routine is fishing in the morning, then, if the weather is sunny, some golf at Ballater in the afternoon, and then more fishing in the long evenings. Royal Deeside is at its incomparably beautiful best in May.

Over the years I have caught many fish there in those perfect 'fly water' pools. Some have been ignominiously shaming – for instance, when I hooked an old wellington boot in the gloaming in Tassach, the bottom pool. I put my rod down and hand-lined it in. It turned into a 6-pound salmon and I have never been allowed to forget it. In my defence, my host John was with me and I suspect we had had a very good dinner, and might not have been in full possession of our faculties.

When things are tough and the fish uninterested in 'normal' flies, you need to try something different. Years ago my parents' generation would simply lob in a prawn, an upstream Devon Minnow or even a worm, often just to catch one for the pot, but most have banned such nefarious tactics. The reason? Because latterly they were used not to catch just one, but to haul in boatloads of fish, all of which were killed by the unscrupulous.

Head boatman here, Malcolm Campbell, is a fan of the skimmer, the sunray shadow, the riffle hitch, dibbling, dry fly or whatever else will tempt them when nothing else will. They are deliberately fished in or on the surface, creating a wake in fast or fastish water. He is brilliant at it and has, more times than I can count, saved a blank day by teaching a novice to skim. It requires concentration, your eye fixed on the wake the fly makes as it meanders across the stream, waiting for the rise, which can be slow and steady, the faintest sip or an explosion of spray and fish. Some leap out and take it on the way down. This is so astonishing that many who have never seen anything like it yank the fly away in shock and anticipation. Alas, often too soon.

In 2006 reports of fish on the Dee were not good, so I begged, borrowed or, more likely, stole a couple of Collie Dog skimmers from Malcolm before setting off to Deeside. We were there for three days. On arrival, nobody had had any action; there were a few fish but they refused to come out to play. After flogging away with traditional flies, we had caught nothing. At 4 p.m. on the last day (why did it take me so long?), my fishing book reliably tells me, I went to Tassach, it was sunny but cold, where one or two salmon had been seen, armed with my Collie Dog skimmers.

About halfway down, as I followed the 'V' in the water that was my fly, a great face appeared, in slow motion, rolled over the top of it in an amazingly leisurely fashion and disappeared back into the water, with my line following it down. I landed that one and immediately afterwards another, it too rolling slowly on the surface with its mouth open where my fly had been. Both were 7 pounds, lovely fish and safely released. Nothing more was doing in Tassach, so I took my new weapon to some of the other pools, or as many as I could fish in the time. I rose four more but none of them took hold.

Consider the facts. Tassach had been fished five times that day (twice by me) with conventional size-10 Cascades, or something similar, before I arrived there at 4 p.m. In addition, nobody had had any pulls or rises in the three days of fishing with four rods, yet I had six 'offers' in just two hours on my 2½-inch Collie Dog skimmer. It was joyful, oh so surprising, and has since become a brilliant addition to my 'all fly' armoury when times are hard.

Why do they sometimes take it when they will take nothing else? Ah, that mystery is part of the joy. Perhaps it annoys them and shakes them out of their indifference. I might not be very good at it, but actually catching one in three or four that come and look at your skimmer or sunray seems to be about right. It does not always work, but when it does . . .

It was some years ago now in Tassach that late afternoon, but so exhilarating. In my mind's eye I can still see those two salmon appearing from the depths, mouths open.

Never on a Sunday

There is one thing that has bugged me for the last sixty years, or however long I have been fishing for salmon. It is illegal (a criminal offence!) in Scotland to fish for migratory fish (i.e. salmon and sea trout) on a Sunday. You can fish for anything else; you can even fish for brown trout in the same river on a Sunday, but you cannot fish for salmon. Even madder, we know now that sea trout and brown trout are the same species, identical, just that one goes to sea and the other does not. But you can fish for one on a Sunday but not the other. Sort that out, if you will, in a court of law. Here in the 2020s you can do almost everything else on a Sunday, but not the peaceful and contemplative pursuit of fishing for salmon. As they say in these parts, 'It's aye been.' It is high time it changed, as it did just over the water in England, many moons ago. This little story of excess demonstrates the point – or not, as the case may be.

It was Thursday, 20 October 1983. It had flooded big time and been unfishable since the 16th, not a line cast, not a fish caught for four days at the peak of the season. At 3 foot 4 inches the river height was too big, but my brother Simon, and friend Simon Wood, were here, having driven through the night from their offices in London. Determined to have a go, they fished all morning for nothing, not a pull. They 'came on' after lunch. I caught one, confined to the bank; the two Simons, alternately rowing each other and then fishing, but in one boat, caught thirteen. A total of fourteen for the top two pools (Cauld stream, 5; Temple Pool, 9).

On Friday the 21st the Simons were over here early, the height 3 foot, big but cleaner than yesterday. Curiously, the Cauld stream yielded nothing but pulls and losses. Sharing one rod, and taking it in turns to row and fish, we caught twenty, all in the Temple Pool: the two Simons, thirteen between them (again); younger brother Mark, three; and my father, three. Again confined to the bank (boo hoo), I caught one.

Saturday the 22nd saw the Simons fishing at dawn, their last day before retreating to 'the smoke' on Sunday. It was 2 foot 9 inches and as clean as a whistle, perfect. I caught six wading, the two Simons twelve between them, brother Mark three and my father two, all from the boat while sharing. Nineteen were caught in the Temple Pool and four in the Cauld stream: twenty-three in total. Fifteen of them were over 10 pounds, 4 over 20 pounds, all fresh from the sea.

Then there was Sunday, of which more later.

On Monday the 24th I went to work after catching a 19-pounder in the Ledges at the top of the Temple Pool. My parents had guests Rosemary and Billy Jepson-Turner staying for a few days. The river height was 2 foot 6 inches, even more perfect. My father rowed his guests all day. She caught six and he twenty, all in the Temple Pool. 'All the fish were fresh, plenty with long-tailed sea lice', according to my fishing book. Billy commented that he would have caught many more if they had not been so big and taken so long to land. Why I stayed in my office all day defies belief, as does my sixty-three-year-old, pretty unfit father rowing all day and netting twenty-six salmon for his guests.

Nowadays, of course, we would have had more rods fishing, and the scores for all those wonderful four days would have been higher. The next day, the 25th, there was a full gale blowing all day and nobody could fish.

So back to that Sunday. With a figure of twenty-three the day before and twenty-seven the day after, it is a no-brainer that

that Sabbath, a sacred non-fishing day apparently, would also have yielded into the twenties. But all we could do was sit and watch. John Knox, or whoever else's outdated religious dogma brought this about, has a lot to answer for. Is it really sacrilegious to fish for salmon on a Sunday, but OK to fish for anything else? Where is the biblical authority for that?

Are we sure that Peter and the other Disciples did not fish on a Sunday? What about the modern working man having only two days at the weekend to fish, and one of them being denied for no good reason? Where is there any sense in it? Of course, ghillies need to have days off, but then allow fishing on Sundays with a stipulation that ghillies and boatmen must be guaranteed a minimum of one day off during the working week, as is the case now but with extensive holidays during the off season.

Where we are now in Scotland is absurd, without either secular or religious rationale for not salmon fishing on Sundays. But will anyone change it?

I doubt it. It's aye been.

Meeting Orri

There is something very British about this tale, and not in a good way. Maybe you could say that we Brits did not understand the seemingly murky world of white-fish quotas. You could say that, but only if you were being charitable. If not, was it that we just do not trust foreigners? That one of them was one of the greatest saviours ever of our salmon makes it so much worse.

I had met Orri Vigfússon before on his many globetrotting visits to drum up support for his mission to halt all high-seas netting of Atlantic salmon. He was a regular visitor to these shores.

This was different. Jeremy Read, director of the Atlantic Salmon Trust, and I found ourselves jetting off to Iceland one May evening in the late 1980s. It was about money, which is why I was asked to go, my accounting skills being required. We landed at midnight, collected by Orri from Keflavík airport and driven to our hotel. It was still daylight, no car headlights, just the occasional sidelight. I remember being surprised by the barrenness, by the rock and laval deposits that dominated the landscape. It was bleak. Not so Orri's welcome.

After breakfast the next day, Orri was on hand again and took us on a tour of his nearby river and a salmon-ranching operation, and generally drove us around showing us the various salmon-related sights. I asked him about the comfortable covering on his car seats. With a broad grin he replied, 'The only good seal is a dead seal!' Icelanders by and large are uncompromising about dealing with anything that gets in the way of, and damages, their traditional way of life: catching fish.

We lunched with the Committee of the North Atlantic Salmon Fund, Orri's very own organisation, which achieved so much, raised prodigious amounts of money and above all persuaded the Greenlanders and Faroese to stop their massive predation of Atlantic salmon. The UK was minded to help but had concerns about the efficacy of some dealings in white-fish quotas. Our job was to be assured that they were open and above board, and report back to potential UK backers. My memory is hazy, but Orri's committee members were both delightful and convincing. We left assured that all was well, slightly shamefaced that we had ever doubted their probity.

Then to Orri's for dinner with his family, Jeremy and I increasingly embarrassed by the hospitality. Well wined and dined, at 11 p.m. I was looking forward to my hotel bed when Orri announced that he had arranged for us all to be flown around Iceland. Of course, why not, if you live in Iceland you sleep in the darkness of winter, and in summer you never go to bed.

He drove us to the small airport at Reykjavík, where we met our pilot, who looked young enough to have only just left school. We clambered hugger-mugger into his small plane, and in no time we had taken off, and were flying up and down Orri's rivers, with him pointing out the best pools, then into the interior where we flew over glaciers and volcanoes (Hekla in particular). I am not the best of fliers and it would be fair to say that by the time we landed on terra firma my nerves were shredded, preferring four Boeing engines to the one, sounding like my lawn-mower, that was the only thing keeping us from falling into Hekla's none-too-welcoming crater. By 2 a.m. I hit the pillow, exhausted but with the unforgettable vision of Iceland's extraordinary scenery, seen from a few thousand feet up in the brooding light of an Arctic summer's night, firmly fixed in my mind. That day had been 31 May, and we left the next morning, 1 June, just as the salmon-fishing season started. How incompetent is that?

Orri was fishing, so we left early for the airport, arriving home via London and Glasgow late that afternoon. I had given Orri a bottle of specially blended whisky. He later reported that he loved it. I gave him more of the same every time I knew I was going to see him in the many years he continued to come to the UK after that.

His mantra, the one we should all adopt, was that he wanted to see 'an abundance of *fiske*' in all our rivers, not just 'enough', but proper abundance. He died in 2017 aged seventy-five. He had suffered from cancer for many years, but I never heard him mention it or complain. A great man, totally dedicated to wild salmon. The fact that there is almost no predation by netting, longlining or whatever other method, either in the high seas or off our shores, is his incomparable legacy to the fish he loved.

The job of saving them is far from complete, but at least now the main player, responsible for killing thousands of tonnes of wild mature salmon in the oceans, man, has left the field of play.

For good. Because of a great Icelander whose probity we had dared to doubt.

The Sea Pool

There is something about a sea pool, the last deep, fresh water of a small river before it enters the sea. In drought conditions, surprisingly common in Scotland in the summer, you can sit there as the tide comes in happily watching the salmon and sea trout leaping about in the sea, impatient to get into the river but unable to do so for lack of water. We used to wade into the sea at Camasunary in Skye and the sea trout would be milling around us in the breakers, often between us and the beach, as we cast our flies in among them. Sea pools are always worth a look, even in the face of expert advice.

There are two sensational rivers in the northwest of Scotland, both named Gruinard, the smaller of the two with 'Little' in front. That they were sensational is not in doubt, maybe less so now with the ever-present curse of fish farms and their sea lice.

We were asked to join a party on the (Big) Gruinard in June 1981, June being too early for large numbers of salmon but 'there should be some, and good for sea trout' in our host's words. The river was low, not many salmon in, but there were sea trout in that long flat pool, the Ironhouse Flats, outside where we were staying, an easy walk after dinner. We were bidden for less than forty-eight hours, and the first day was spent happily exploring the river and its pools, but it was very low, and few salmon had managed to make it in. That evening we tried the Ironhouse Flats. Some sea trout were caught but I was blank. Nobody had touched a salmon all day.

Ever hopeful and curious, I had spoken to the ghillie about going down to the sea, by Gruinard House, as the tide was coming in. He was gloomy, implying I was wasting my time and anyway high tide was at dawn the next day, not worth getting up that early, he said. I had recced the sea pool that evening, quite short with the tide out, but if you were there just as the sea water came in, there must be a chance as the salmon had been unable to get in for some weeks now. They would be desperate.

I woke at dawn, incredibly early in northern Scotland in mid-June, crept out of the house and strolled the half-mile to the sea pool as dawn broke. I was too early, but not by much, and I could see the tide advancing, wave by wave. Some fish were jumping far out to sea and, as the tide reached the sea pool, there were the unmistakable bow waves of fish coming in.

There was a slight stream, but it slowed to nothing as it hit the oncoming tide. I cast and then hand-lined my No. 10 Munro Killer into the, by now, flat calm pool. I was expecting nothing, but suddenly the fly was grabbed by a silver bullet that shot out to sea, heading for America, and for a minute or two I could see no reason why it should not get there. After ten minutes of hard graft, I had it, a perfect 8-pounder covered in long-tailed sea lice, as all salmon are when they first come in from the sea, and beached it among the seaweed. That ten minutes had lost vital fishing time, the pool by now almost wholly subsumed into the ocean. It looked hopeless but I had a few more casts, fish still showing, handlining fast to attract attention and it did: another one took, this time 5 pounds and again it set off out to sea. By the time it lay in the seaweed at my feet, it was too late to try any more, the sea pool now part of the ocean and unrecognisable.

I could hardly believe it had happened, so dire had been the ghillie's predictions. I strolled back up the river, trying the little pools on the way, thinking at least one of those many salmon must have made it in. But there was no sign; it was just too low.

I arrived back for breakfast with my two fish, which I left with our hosts, for they were there for the rest of the week. There was some surprise at my success and we left before seeing the ghillie who had been so discouraging.

The morals of the story are, I suppose, those age-old ones: 'The early bird . . .' and 'If you don't try . . .' But perhaps, with fishing, 'You just never know.' A large part of why we bother.

Smoke Gets in Your Eyes

The Carron near Bonar Bridge on Scotland's east coast is a lovely river, but tiny compared to the Tweed. I have been lucky enough to fish it with friends many times over the years, often successfully, but never more so than on this occasion, or at least not in so short a time. 'Friends', given their behaviour in this instance, is a comparative term. I got my own back.

'Bastards!' I cried as I shut the door on the School House sitting room, my bedroom for the night. We had arrived at Gruinards on the Carron that evening, halfway through the week. The 'oldies' had the first half of the week. The river had been low and they had caught little. It was April 1988 and the Carron needs water to get the spring salmon moving upstream, and taking a fly.

The party comprised David and Nigel Houldsworth, cousins, and John Carson. John is the only man I know who hooked and landed a salmon on the back cast, on the Tweed in our Cauld stream in the autumn, the fish taking his fly as it touched the water behind him. I know. I was the boatman.

Now when four old friends meet, hotfoot from their various offices, pink tickets from wives and families, things can get lively, especially on the first evening. Too late, we decided the jollity must stop and our beds beckoned. Then and only then was I told that my billet was in the sitting room where we had been relaxing, drinking and where both David and John had been smoking cigars. Hence my outburst. Have you ever tried sleeping in a room filled with cigar smoke? Despite windows being thrown open, the smell lingers and I could not sleep as a result. I tossed and turned, cursing my 'friends'.

It had been raining when we arrived, so there was hope that the river would be up in the morning. At 6 a.m. I had had enough of not sleeping, got up and drove down to the river as noisily as possible, hoping to wake the others. The Carron was up 6 inches, not much but enough for an hour or so before it would start dropping. I tried the tail of that great pool, the Morail, but it was not quite big enough, so I moved down to the Kennel Run.

I had caught many fish in my time in the lovely Gruinards pools, thanks largely to the generosity of the then owner Jean Matterson, but never in the Kennel Run. It had always seemed the wrong height, too big and they go straight through it, too low and there is not enough depth to hold them. But that morning as I approached it looked perfect, and I saw a salmon jump as I waded into the neck. The whole pool was under a hundred yards long, so I would fish it quickly before moving onto the better pools near Gruinard House, and then back for breakfast and some stern words with my friends about cigars.

I had on a small black-and-orange tube fly and a sinking tip. In an hour, I caught four sparkling silver spring salmon and lost another. My book says they weighed 12, 8, 8 and 6 pounds. I noticed the rocks that had been submerged when I arrived were beginning to show above water as the river dropped. It was all over.

Nigel ('Big Nige', don't ask!) appeared on the bank and when I told him I had caught four, he said, 'Oh, well done', through gritted teeth, for he had hoped to get to the river first, but had overslept, not having the benefit of thick cigar smoke as a bedfellow. And that was it. The river fell quickly, back to its previous all-too-low level, and no more fish were caught.

All of which brought to mind the words of Jerome Kern's and Otto Harbach's song 'Smoke Gets in Your Eyes' and its pertinent comments about 'laughing friends', tears and smiles. Whenever I hear that marvellous song, it reminds me of a magical hour on the Carron that would never have happened without smoke getting in my eyes; I would have arrived too late. And I still cannot stand the lingering aftermath of cigars.

The Opposite Test

We have known Mark and Tina Clarfelt for so long that I cannot remember when we first went to Linhay Meads. Their hospitality knows no bounds, the house is gloriously comfortable, and a carrier of the Test runs through the garden. The main River Test and yet more carriers, all bearing trout, are but a short walk away across the meadow. It is heaven.

As boys, my brothers and I learned dry-fly fishing on the Don at Grandhome. Somehow the Test is different: unique, stunningly beautiful and English to its core. The most striking difference from salmon rivers, where you cast methodically for most of the day, is that the actual fishing bit on a chalk stream can be surprisingly limited.

Some maths buff will have worked out that there is a direct correlation between how much you flog away for salmon, and how many you catch. That correlation could well be the inverse, the exact opposite, for dry fly on the Test. In short, the less you flog away, the more you catch. Time spent just sitting, watching and taking in the scenery at Linhay Meads can be surprisingly productive. Above all, you are looking for the telltale dimple of a rising trout, and, if wise, you will wait, watching for even longer, until it becomes a regular feeder and just that much easier to deceive with your dry fly imitation.

We play 9 holes at Leckford in the morning, then call in at the tackle shop in Stockbridge, Messrs Robjents, with a most persuasive proprietor, to replenish with mayfly, flotant,* etc., for the afternoon and evening sport. It can be a struggle, after lunch and

---

* A substance to help dry flies to float.

light refreshments, to avoid a short afternoon kip. Then down to the river for as long as you like. I have been known to be late for dinner at around 9 p.m. if the trout are rising but nobody minds. One late evening I was broken by a very big wild brownie, well over 5 pounds, as it buried itself among the overhanging roots on the far bank in the fading light. I could do nothing with it, despite 6-pound nylon, so strong I assumed it was wild, as opposed to the less energetic stocked variety. The real kudos is in catching trout under 1 pound, for they too must be wild. Nothing that small is stocked.

There are pike, and big ones, not good for the brownies, which become pike lunch. Mark suspected something when a particularly productive pool, unkindly called Duffers' Corner, appeared to have no trout in it. His garish, very large fly and wire trace leader were expertly cast into the most likely spots, and the resulting explosion of a pike in attack mode confirmed his suspicions, as he finally dragged the 12-pound killing machine into the net.

There are several carriers as well as the main river, all productive to fish, and such fun to go seeking trout in the less likely places. One such is jokingly and grandly called 'The House Water' a carrier running away from the house and into the woods, not easy fishing among the nettles and overhanging trees, but a triumph and bragging rights if you catch one. I had a 3-pound bream one evening, the most perfect specimen, if disappointing in the fighting stakes. It rolled over and gave up almost as soon as it was hooked.

I fondly recall a Saturday with rain and cold in late May – not good, you would think, for mayfly. The other guests did not brave the conditions for long. I had the river to myself, and lost count of the trout I caught, at least twenty and all released unharmed for another day. For some reason, the mayfly were everywhere when at other times in similar cold they would have stayed at home.

On a normal Hampshire summer's day, the sheer joy of strolling along the riverbank is, on its own, reward enough, no matter the obvious excellence of the fishing. I take my time, there is no hurry, sitting and waiting in the sun, then in the shade, mixed with gently wandering and all the time in search of a feeding trout. The water is so clear that with the right light you can see the trout holding position behind some weed, or close in under the bank, and try for them even if they are not rising. If they come, slowly emerging from the depths, at your fly, it is mesmerising, waiting for the mouth to shut before tightening. The whole experience is a joy and the opposite of what I am used to, flogging away for salmon on the Tweed, with far too little time to sit and consider.

From the cold and gloom of a mid-January afternoon as this is being written, thoughts of idling distractedly, rod in hand, on one of those little riverside seats beside the Test at Linhay Meads, is the stuff of dreams.

Fishing Bores

I hope the PC police will take this with a large pinch of salt. The few times I met that legendary salmon fisherman John Ashley-Cooper, he was most reluctant to talk about fishing, even though he did little else; maybe that was why. What follows is a bit of fun, but those who talk about it too much are out there. I don't think I am one of them.

Forgive, if you can, the misogynistic tone, but some things need to be said. First, let me say that I am a very lucky man. My wife has put up with me, I think reasonably happily, for over forty years. She dislikes fishing, and used to dislike golf. This was and is a good thing, because it has not escaped my attention that women can become fanatical about one or other and – heaven forfend – some both. They become obsessed and, worse, cannot stop talking about it.

As you will no doubt by now be aware, I am a salmon fisherman through and through. But – and it is a vital but – I do not talk about it, or at least not that much. Long ago I spotted the glazed look that quickly came over the eyes of the attempted chatted-up 'girlfriend-to-be'. Most people find fishing stories staggeringly dull, and they give not one toss how many you caught or what cripplingly dull fly you caught it on.

A while ago now (the pain has dulled somewhat), we were out to dinner and met for the first time a couple who had just moved to the Borders. The charming wife was sitting between my old friend Nigel and me. Things were going swimmingly until Nigel uttered the fateful words, 'Do tell my old mate Andrew what you know about salmon fishing. Poor fellow hasn't done much and longs to

103

know more about it.' Being new to the area, she did not know that this was gigantically untrue.

Well, not knowing her at all well, fatally I hesitated in telling her that I knew more about it than Izaak Walton in his pomp, not that said Izaak knew much, preferring the art of angling with a frog: not the weapon of choice for salmon.

Off she went, giving me the benefit of her advice on the noble art, and twenty minutes later I was still giving it the 'Oh really?!' to everything she said, while odious Nigel was killing himself laughing and adding fuel to the fire by suggesting to her, 'Do tell him about the day when you caught three salmon at Mertoun.' I had been done like a kipper, and it was far too late to say that there was literally nothing she could tell me that I did not already know. I could only go on pretending that it was all news to me. I have never had a more exasperating dinner, nor Nigel a more satisfactory one. He takes the greatest pleasure in recounting the sorry tale at every possible opportunity, over and over again to anyone who will listen, invariably within my earshot so that he can witness the involuntary shudder at the memory of it all.

Women are so competitive. Girlfriends and wives like catching more and bigger fish than their male counterparts and if anyone mentions pheromones, I shall scream. Of course women catch more and bigger fish than men, because decent fellows allow them to fish the best pools first, with hot and cold running boatmen or ghillies, while we trudge off alone to the furthest pool, fishing Siberia, where the last one caught was by some bloke called Ashley-Cooper, to his surprise, in 1963.

I recall one such at Knockando on the Spey, fishing in a big party as guests of Martin and Catherine Wills in the 1980s. We men had done a bit of it, but Martin, the perfect host, kept putting one of the girls in the best places, with the lovely Sandys as ghillie. Until then, she had never fished. After a few sessions of us not catching much and the novice always having success, she issued the never-to-be-forgotten line one evening before dinner: 'I can't understand why none of you are catching anything!' We blokes made a pact, a solemn bond, to strangle her at the next available opportunity.

I am spared all this with a wife who thinks that fish are both slimy and smelly, best avoided at all times. Even the well-heeled aficionados of the pristine Harrods Food (and Fish) Hall might concede she has a point.

But here's the rub. Against all the odds, whereas ten years ago Jane put golf in the same bin as fishing, now she is fanatical about hitting that little white ball, endlessly obsessing about why she cannot get out of bunkers. My advice not to go into them in the first place appears not to help. If pushed, and to save myself from endless vitriol and potential outrage from half my readership, I will admit that most bores about golf and fishing are men. I just do not normally sit next to them at dinner.

Jane does.

The Price of Principles

We all feel strongly about things. This is a tale of those who know what those 'things' are and would make mischief, have fun even, at our expense. You have to be on your guard: one slip and pariah status, via social media, beckons. Pictures are especially dangerous. This was written one beautiful July day just after nearly falling into the trap.

Sally Yonge, the far better half of Nick Yonge, ex both fish farmer and CEO of the River Tweed Commission, caught her first salmon here on Saturday, a magnificent 11-pound fresh cock fish, taught and rowed by redoubtable ghillie Bruce. She then appeared triumphantly, with the very dead fish, at an outdoor fundraising lunch we were having here for Marie Curie. Congratulated by all, she was photographed with her prize, a great moment and maybe the start of a future fishing career.

Need one say, those who I barely class as friends thought it would be amusing – indeed they could scarcely contain their joy at the idea – to take a photo of yours truly alongside the dead 11-pounder and the spinning rod and whatever ghastly lure was to blame. The issue, of course, being that I dislike both spinning and killing fish, so the opportunity to picture me with the incriminating evidence of both, in one shot, was almost too much for my so-called friends to bear. That Sally had never fished before, that the river was big and murky, and that this was her first salmon, all of these things would have been absent in a picture of me with a dead fish and spinning rod. Pictures may indeed paint a thousand words, but in this case they would have been the wrong ones.

My antennae being in tip-top shape, and my brain in mid-season form, you will be disappointed to hear that those budding David Baileys were destined to fail. There is no such photo any-where; had there been, exile and temporary leave of absence from these shores would have been the price. Can you imagine the Twitter storm?

So traumatised was I by all this that an instant antidote was the only cure. I ventured out, after tea when all was quiet and the many lunch guests had gone. I took my 15-foot rod, an intermediate line and a smallish bright-yellow fly, to the Ledges at the top of the Temple. Despite a gale and not really being able to see my feet for the colour in the water, I hooked and landed a bright 8-pounder. After unhooking it most expertly and rapidly, the fish never leaving the water, I sent it on its way with a silent 'God speed'.

I feel sure that salmon winked at me as we looked each other in the eye, while the hook was being prised from its scissors.* It gave a parting *thwack* of its tail as it slid into the depths. I breathed a huge sigh of relief; normal service had been resumed.

All was well in my world. No dead fish, no spinning rod, but then my 'friends' would not have been interested in a photo of all that fly-fishing stuff and a salmon being released safely back into the water. Friends? Some friends.

---

* Where the salmon's upper and lower jaws meet.

No Way to Treat a Noble Fish

Some will say what follows is rubbish. They would catch and kill as many salmon as they could, all in the name of sport, regardless of method. They, and their forebears, are the whole reason that the Atlantic salmon is so endangered now. Selfish and ignorant disregard for the wider picture, of a uniquely precious resource, by too many of us humans has led to this. As the only remaining permitted exploiters in Scotland of such an iconic species, we river managers and anglers have the ultimate responsibility. There is nobody else to blame. How we conduct ourselves – and what we now do to protect our wonderful salmon – is how we shall be judged. We are in the endgame. We cannot afford to fail, for the salmon's sake.

If only I were more articulate. If only I could express how I feel. If onlys – I have loads of them. An attempt at any form of expression tends to come out as a rant, and is dismissed as such.

I despair at the ignorance and myopia of those who should know better, especially governments, for it is only governments who have the ultimate power to effect change. Why has our Atlantic-salmon population been allowed to decline by two-thirds, by three-quarters, by 90 per cent – who knows how severe the loss? At a time when our own nets, the North East Drift nets, the other Scottish and English river and coastal nets, the Faroese, the Greenlanders, Uncle Tom Cobley and all, were catching and killing thousands of tonnes of salmon in the 1960s and 1970s, there were still plenty left over for the anglers to catch. All of those nets have gone, and yet there are still barely enough fish to populate our rivers.

River managers have done their best by removing physical in-river obstructions and by buying off all nets, but that has been to deal only with the symptoms, not the underlying disease. There is something chronically wrong in the salmon world, and we have yet to tackle it. We have been tinkering around the edges. The disease, the underlying cause, is climate change and our ever warming world. It is so blindingly obvious but anyone suggesting it is accused of overthinking it, of over-dramatisation, even anthropomorphism.

The salmon likes cold water, and not only are the oceans heating up but, crucially, so are our rivers. At water temperatures of over 70°F, which we get now in the Tweed, salmon are not happy. At over 80°F they begin to die. Predictions of temperature rises tend to deal in averages, not spikes. An average rise in temperature of 1.5 or 2°C will inevitably involve spikes far higher than that. Our fish could die, the vital young ones in particular, and in large numbers. Can we do anything to stop it? In a macro sense, maybe global warming can be halted and reversed, but it will take time. What we can do is indulge in massive riparian tree planting. Quite simply, we shall be able to halt global warming only slowly. The sun will continue to shine ever stronger, but what we can do is provide shade along the Tweed's huge and diverse 'track', its precious tributaries, all those thousands of kilometres of them. It has started, thanks to the Tweed Forum. I will not live to see it, but if I could come back in thirty years' time, I would hope to see our uplands, especially our riparian uplands, as wooded as they once were over three hundred years ago, before we humans cut them all down.

Which brings me to my fellow anglers and Tweed fishery proprietors. As the guardians of our fish, the only 'exploiters' left standing, it is our solemn duty to protect our fish. That includes a code of behaviour that recognises the privilege we have of being allowed to fish for them. There is no longer even a pretence that we are fishing to catch salmon for food. Most rivers see over 90 per cent of the catch released. We are fishing for sport, nothing else. Any angler who now says he is going fishing to catch a salmon to kill and eat is being extraordinarily disingenuous, not only unaware of his own motives but of the amount of farmed salmon in the supermarkets. Why on earth would you kill a wild salmon given the dangers they face?

Along with that realisation, that we are fishing for sport alone, comes the responsibility to fish in a way that is the most sporting. There has to be a degree of challenge involved for the required level of sporting satisfaction, as well as a respect for our endangered and magnificent quarry. That so many anglers think that it is remotely acceptable to spin endlessly, all day often, for salmon, cooped up in low water in our pools, with an upstream flying condom, or whatever other dreadful lure, is a matter of the utmost shame to our angling community. It is certainly the biggest kick in the teeth possible to all those traditional netsmen whose livelihoods have been extinguished to allow anglers like us to have some salmon to fish for. I have often wondered if the unstoppable progress towards removing all netting of wild salmon, and its universal support from anglers, was motivated by personal, selfish interest, of the 'I will catch more fish if there are no nets' variety, or by any genuine concerns for the survival of the species.

In my world, we would be planting trees in their millions in our headwaters, not killing any salmon that we catch and allowing only fly fishing. No longer is it humans that matter; it is the fish. We have screwed it up big time for our salmon over the last few decades, even centuries. In every action we take now, the fish and their survival are paramount.

It is the only way to have any chance of eventual success. It will take a long time.

What Life Is This?

I have been troubled all my life by mild obsession, and although fishing should be the most relaxing and joyous of sports, for some, perhaps even most, it can become obsessive, with nowhere near enough time given to 'smelling the roses'. Or at least not until we become older. This was written while contemplating the joys of the Test.

Our relationship with salmon catch numbers is complex and, for most of us, very far from consistent. To catch a salmon every cast has been described as a definition of hell. We hear stories from Russia of single rods catching 200 salmon in a week. Is that acceptable? What is the point, when you release them all anyway? There is the whiff of wanton cruelty in catching more to no purpose, but if you killed them, you would be vilified for slaughter, the antithesis of sport.

Attitude is affected by age. The older we get, the more we empathise with our quarry; flogging away just to catch one more becomes less appealing, while we take the extra time to reflect how lucky we are to be able to smell those roses and appreciate the beauty of the river: the kingfisher, the otter, the osprey, the baby ducks. And we tend to spend longer in the hut at lunchtime.

For many, certainly the more mature anglers, a salmon in the morning and another after lunch, with a couple more pulls, is the perfect day. We incline more to the words of William Henry Davies (1871–1940) in his poem *Leisure*:

> What is this life if, full of care,
> We have no time to stand and stare.
>
> No time to stand beneath the boughs
> And stare as long as sheep or cows.

> No time to see, when woods we pass,
> Where squirrels hide their nuts in grass.
>
> No time to see, in broad daylight,
> Streams full of stars, like skies at night.
>
> No time to turn at Beauty's glance,
> And watch her feet, how they can dance.
>
> No time to wait till her mouth can
> Enrich that smile her eyes began.
>
> A poor life this if, full of care,
> We have no time to stand and stare.

But, and here's the rub, we still like to hear of the big scores. The most visited pages by far on fishing websites are the daily catches pages. 'Wark 30 again!' stressed executives in London text, dreaming of magical days away from the daily grind and surrounded by leaping salmon. Dreams are what the Tweed and other salmon rivers are selling, and for that there have to be catch numbers, just as the South of France has to have sunshine.

Among the contradictions in our attitudes to numbers, there is one stereotype who deserves our sympathy. Is there perhaps something of that figure in all of us? The drug that keeps us all coming back is the 'pull', that magical moment when contact is made, on a fly of course, and some cannot get enough. Uncontrolled, as with all addictions, it leads to obsession and unhappiness.

These musings come from the beguiling and beautiful Hampshire Test in May, scribbled in between a good deal of what William Henry Davies was on about. The mayfly, as with everything this year, are late.

Dogs, We've Had a Few

Ever since coming to live here in 1981, we have had dogs as companions and friends. It started with Fergus ('Fungle Bungle') and now we have Poppy ('Puppsie') and Roxy ('The Rocket'). Whatever we start out calling our dogs, their names change as if by magic. They are invariably messy and smelly, and they eat, and roll in, disgusting things, but we love them and they all have very different characters.

When we married in 1980, Jane's border terrier, Fergus, almost came down the aisle with her. He was incredibly brave when barking and growling at other dogs, but only when securely on a lead or from within the car. He was followed by a succession of girls; we have never had a boy since. There was golden retriever Saffron ('Saffy'), the most beautiful and charming dog you could ever meet. Jane had her painted for me. So successful was Saffy that we acquired another golden retriever, Sarah ('Bugger off, Sarah'). She was a mistake. We never had another retriever.

Then there was Scruffy ('Scumbag'). She was a long-haired Jack Russell (hunt) terrier. Her mother's nose had been bitten off by foxes. We went to pick up little Scruffy from the hunt kennels. Jane had spoken by phone to someone called Jeff Cock. Mr Jeffcock was quite surprised at being addressed as 'Mr Cock' when Jane knocked on his door. One of the children immediately said that Scruffy looked just like a Scumbag, and so she was. She was uncompromisingly aggressive if you touched a particular spot on the top of her head, and she strutted around as if she owned the place, which she did. If worried she had lost me, she would swim out into the middle of the mighty Tweed while we were fishing from a boat.

A little white head would appear at the end of the boat, midstream, from which she would be plucked, completely unabashed, and proceed to soak us all by shaking herself dry. She swam the Tweed to the other bank once, convinced the person on the other side was me. We lost her for a couple of hours and worried that she had been run over on the Wark road. Eventually someone rang from Wark saying they had a Jack Russell sitting in their best armchair. When I went to collect her, she didn't move or wag her tail; it was a rebuke for losing her.

When she died, the family mourning was intense. We had lost a great friend and a terrifyingly strong character. Son Richard in his wedding speech said, 'Quite honestly, Scumbag was a better parent to Nick and me than either of our real parents', to surprised gasps and slightly nervous laughter. I rather think he meant it.

Next there was Pickles, a terrier-cross mongrel, the brightest of them all, but she died young from some horrible swallowing deformity.

My brothers and I had given my father Tully, a beautifully trained and quiet six-year-old yellow Labrador, as company after my mother died. He had not wanted a dog and was initially quite cross when we disobeyed him. After a week or two of having Tully, he wrote us the nicest and most moving letter. It still brings a tear to my eye whenever I re-read it. 'Tully has been the most astonishing success,' he wrote, 'and I am sorry I was so lukewarm to start with.' We inherited Tully ('Tulls') when he died a few months after writing that letter. We then had her and Susie ('Soozles Poozles'), a Lancashire Heeler, Jane's biggest defender. She would bite you if you touched, kissed or in any way got too close. She was a lovely dog and bore her old age with great dignity.

Now we have 'The Rocket', a dizzy, dumb blonde, broken-coated (how grand is that!), unaggressive(!) Jack Russell. Everyone loves her. And 'Puppsie', another Lancashire Heeler. In the eyes of my children, Puppsie is almost in the Scumbag league so far as affection and character are concerned. She is permanently on the lookout, on patrol, ears cocked, intent on repelling boarders, endlessly barking and aggressive at distance, until she meets someone, when the tail starts wagging and she is all over them like a rash. There are some dogs she simply cannot stand, mainly Border terriers, and how she lets them know. She hates the postman's van with an irreconcilable passion.

Will we get any more after 'The Rocket' and 'Puppsie' are gone, if we outlive them? They are a tie, but also amazing company and endlessly amusing.

A house without dogs? The jury, as ever, is out.

Summer's End

I have only once seen a therapist. Jane and I saw him after
Freddie died, for half a dozen sessions, no more. I was pre-
scribed antidepressants but, being sensitive to most brands, did
not take them for long. I objected to being 'depressed', but
never minded being told I suffered from 'anxiety'; indeed, I
told the doctors the latter was the right diagnosis. Maybe medi-
cally the two were seen as the same back then; they certainly
were not to me.

Ian Graham, my partner at work, died of cancer at the end of 1989,
so I was running two offices not one, had borrowed heavily both for
the business and to build our house, was paying school fees for the
older boys, and so on. I did little but work, no time for anything
else. The situation was described to me then as a bottle of milk that
had gradually become fuller and fuller, until it was permanently
flowing over the rim. 1989 and 1990 were bad, a classic case of
overwork and overcommitment, indeed over-everything.

Freddie had died at six weeks old, a tragedy of such indescrib-
able proportions that I can still recall every tiny detail of what
happened before and after – holding his little lifeless body, his
body-switch turned off; rushing up to the Cottage Hospital; the
doctors trying to save him; and, finally, his tiny white coffin. It
was thirty-two years ago now, on Saturday 27 January 1990 at
12 a.m. I still have in my wallet the paper I was writing, for work,
of course, when I heard Jane. I later wrote the heading 'Freddie
Douglas-Home' and on the other side: 'I stopped writing here
when Freddie died', with a note of the date and the precise time
of Jane's screams.

I don't know how Jane bore it; she became very ill. I am sure she remembers it as if it were yesterday. She thinks of Freddie every day.

Neither of us is comfortable answering the question how many children do we have? 'Three' inevitably leads to questions about Freddie and consequent awkwardness for the questioner, whereas 'two' is somehow a denial of Freddie. We try to say three. If we are not that keen on the person asking the questions, we deliberately say two because somehow, silly though it is, we want to protect Freddie, to keep him to ourselves.

As I write, it is the end of November, and shortly, on both 13 December (his birthday) and 27 January, we will go and see him in Cornhill's churchyard. The lettering is fading on his headstone. He has lain all alone there for thirty-two years.

Jane and I have booked the plots on either side of his little grave.

AUTUMN

For most of my life, until 2014 to be precise, the Tweed's autumn run of salmon and grilse was extraordinary. Year after year, in the period following 14 September when the commercial nets stopped fishing, there would be massive runs of bright beautiful autumn fish, often coinciding with the seasonal rains swelling the river to allow them to move upstream fast. We took it for granted, until it was no longer there. It was the brightest part of my least favourite season, with the gloom and darkness of encroaching winter just around the corner.

The year 2010 produced the crowning glory of those big autumns. The numbers now seem almost inconceivable. By the end of July that year, the Lees had caught just 82 salmon in six months, with zero – not a single salmon – caught in April. August contributed another eighty-one before all hell let loose with 233 in September, 322 in October and 213 in November, for a grand sum of 931 salmon. On Monday 27 September, a total of sixty-one salmon, all on a fly, was caught by four and a half rods, the half being me and son Richard who fished for a total of three hours in the worst pool, the Annay, which we keep for ourselves (we caught six). One of the tenants, Francis Sidoli, caught twenty-three. It would be no surprise if that total of sixty-one should have been more. As most of the fish were released, there could be no body count. Remembering exactly what you caught and where – when, for example, Francis caught seventeen in the afternoon in one pool – was no exact science. Annoyingly, I had damaged my neck and could hardly fish that autumn, but it enables me to claim, 'We would have reached a thousand if I had been fit and well.' What is certainly true is that much of the two miles here was unfished, because so much time was taken up playing and landing salmon in the best pools. How phlegmatic we should be that our November catches had dropped to single figures by 2018, and have stayed there since, is a matter for debate. Some say it is just cyclical and appear to have no issue with such dramatic decline. I am far from convinced it is that simple.

In my own autumn, from say forty to sixty years old, I cannot remember a whole lot as life stayed pretty much the same, although it was indeed gradually and imperceptibly changing. As well as winding down my accountancy career, I became very involved with Sir Walter Scott's house at Abbotsford, did a stint of eight years as Chairman of the River Tweed Commissioners and continued living in an ever growing house as my sons, Richard and Nicholas, morphed into young men of considerable stature (in every way).

If I have a regret it is that I did not enjoy things enough, but then after Freddie's death, joy was often absent.

A Great Fishing Hotel

Traditional Scottish fishing hotels from the 1950s to 1990s were never luxurious. They resembled old gentlemen's clubs, warm and comforting, log fires ablaze everywhere. The barman knew your name and would ask, 'Your usual, sir?', which made you feel so at home, despite the fading grandeur, the slightly smelly chair covers and the ill-fitting carpets and curtains. Hot water there had to be, because the fishermen and women were cold after a day on the river. The bedrooms and beds were OK; you had to put up with them for only a few nights. Those were the days of going to Scotland to fish for a week, the same party and the same time every year. And there were fish to be caught, the public demonstration of which was the tens of laid-out silver bodies inside the hotel's hall, with labels attached, identifying which beat and which captor had been successful. If you did that now, killing all you catch and demonstrating the fact so publicly, the online trolls would eat you for breakfast and shameful exile to a modern-day Alcatraz would be the safest option. How things have changed in a generation! What follows is all about a prime example of one of those great hotels of yore in its slightly faded glory. We shall never see their like again.

The Revd Robert Parker – the richest vicar in the land, some say – has bought the Ednam House Hotel in Kelso. Not the opening plot line of an Agatha Christie, crucially lacking Miss Marples' waspish observational skills and Colonel Prothero's inevitable demise in *Murder at the Vicarage*. Nonetheless, in Tweedside's fishing circles this is both red-hot and slightly shocking news.

Nothing is ever supposed to change in the Borders, you see. More often than not it never does, so that when it does, we Borderers sit up and take note.

Many think of the Ednam House as an old overcoat: slightly careworn, by no means in the first flush, but curiously warm and comforting, never pretentious, an old friend, still handsome but, in the nicest possible way, having seen better days.

I had two uncles who frequented its bar, both prone to slotting in there around noon for a G&T or two while shopping was being done and errands run by the driver, usually a long-suffering and accommodating wife; then back home for lunch.

One such uncle, Major Henry Douglas-Home, my father's second-eldest brother, kept a caged mynah bird named Gluck, a superlative, incorrigible and wicked mimic. Gluck was stationed in the sitting room at Old Greenlaw, and the major was wont to pass judgement on Gluck's unwarranted interjections, when nobody else was there, by saying in admonishment and to shut up the irksome fowl, 'Fuck off, Gluck.'

The inevitable consequence, of course, being that the evil Gluck, when the major and my Aunt Felicity were entertaining the great and the good to afternoon tea, in any lull in the conversation, or just after a guest had been asked whether they liked lemon or milk in their tea, would pipe up with a most shrill and piercing rendition of the major's favourite phrase, 'Fuck off, Gluck!' Old ladies were known to faint at this sudden and unexpected assault on their very considerable sensibilities by the mynah, much to the major's quiet satisfaction. My mother was never that keen on Uncle Henry ever since he had toured around a cocktail party in the 1960s identifying her as Christine Keeler to anyone who did not know her already.

The other uncle, Captain Billy Straker-Smith, was my mother's only sibling, the most delightful of men, if with some very human failings, principally related to both gambling and the sauce that the Ednam House barman served up at 12 noon daily.

He introduced me to the Honourable Company of Edinburgh Golfers at Muirfield, where one day in the locker room I was approached by a member.

'Who is that man you are with?' he asked.

I answered with Billy's name and number, to which he replied, 'Good Lord, do you know that he told me he put £5,000 on my horse Rubstic to win the 1979 Grand National at 12 to 1 and won £60,000? Can that be so? Because that was far more than I put on it.'

'Sadly,' I responded, 'it could be all too true, but I fear it gives you some idea how much he loses.'

Later, Billy had to sell and lease back his thousand-acre Carham estate to settle his gambling debts to the White Elephant Club in Curzon Street and no doubt numerous other London-based houses of chance.

Possessed of a wonderful turn of phrase and a commanding put-down, and troubled by a tiresome, loquacious vicar (not the Revd Parker) at River Tweed Commission meetings when he was chairman, Captain Billy would politely hear the vicar out and then simply say, 'Thank you, padre', without ever allowing any further discussion by the assembled company of the point the good padre had been making.

I digress. Back to the matter at hand.

Over many decades, Ednam House has been synonymous with middle Tweed fishing, either side of Kelso, with pictures galore of dead fish laid out in the hall, and salmon fishers young and old milling around discussing the triumphs and disasters of their day, the stories becoming ever more exaggerated as the barman warms to his task of refuelling his customers, long into the evening.

The hotel's position, overlooking the Tweed just below the junction of the Tweed and the Teviot, is perfect and only slightly spoiled in its outward aspect by the extraordinarily functional but far from beautiful Pavilion on the Kelso showground. It looks its very best from the south side of the Tweed, looking back towards the town, with the bridge on your right and the Junction Pool to the left.

The Brooks family have run it as a hotel since 1928, four generations starting and ending with a Ralph, and for most of my life run by Alistair, himself an expert, keen and peripatetic salmon fisher. It would have been perfect had they ever owned the Junction fishing, right on the hotel's doorstep, their chance coming and going when Roxburghe Estates sold the Junction to the Miller family in the 1970s.

So what of the future for such a well-loved hotel? I have stayed at Doxford Hall Hotel, another in Padre Parker's stable, and you would think, if Doxford Hall is any guide, that changes are afoot at the Ednam House. Sadly, for the long-time residents and those who, like my uncles, treated it as an old friend, it is unlikely to be the same. Of course, change must happen and some significant investment is needed.

In a funny way, despite improvements, we shall have lost something special, and we shall miss the old girl just as she was, with all her shortcomings, with Alistair Brooks sitting in his chair by the bar welcoming one and all. Instead, I fear we shall get just another hotel.

Misplaced nostalgia, you will say, but somehow both Kelso and middle Tweed salmon fishing will never be the same.

Lunch

I gave up shooting many years ago, mainly because I enjoyed the lunches more than the shooting. With fishing, both are equally enjoyable with the coming together after a morning on the river, a chance to swap experiences among friends, to compare notes and to tease each other whenever possible. Lunch is not why we all go salmon fishing with friends, but it's a big part of it. I hope this will show you what I mean.

Salmon fishing usually takes place among friends; we go as a party of mates, or as a member of a syndicate or club. Of course, we meet strangers along the way, on the riverbank, but by and large we occupy a little world, a bubble of our own, when fishing. That is how we like it. It is part of the attraction, to relax, to lose ourselves in the act of fishing, in beautiful surroundings, and with those we know well.

It does not always work out like that.

'Ave, piscator,' said the aged Oxford don, distractedly, no doubt contemplating some Euclidean puzzle, meandering along the banks of the Test, trout rod in hand, waiting for the mayfly to hatch and for the trout to start lunch.

He could not have known that his proposed interlocutor, also strolling if slightly more purposefully, coming towards him, in search of the same feeding trout, was by origin Glaswegian, definitely made good, but as Pete and Dud used to put it, he 'did not have the Latin'.

Long experience had taught said Glaswegian that any word with 'pis' required an immediate, robust response, and before he could factor in the unlikelihood of being abused by the kindly-looking elderly fellow angler coming towards him, his rapier riposte, knee-jerk no doubt, was 'And fuck off yourself too, Jimmy', much to the aged don's consternation and surprise, as they both continued on their opposite paths.

Chris Tarrant, keen and expert salmon angler, prompted by one of the Junction boatmen, where he was fishing, told the story of the well-heeled fisherman, corpulent, red-faced, plutocratic, and, worst of all, clearly English, in the boat just above the Kelso bypass bridge, fishing Hempsford Pool.

Above them on the bypass bridge, there appeared a youth pushing an empty supermarket trolley. What would happen next was plain for all to see, but, against the advice of the boatman, who knew the cause was lost, the fat fisherman laid aside his rod, stood up in the boat, the better to project his voice, and started to reason with the youth above him on the bridge.

'My dear young man, I beg you not to do it. Think of the environmental consequences, the cost to the supermarket, the need to collect the trolley wherever it lodges downstream, wherever it ends up after the next flood. What about the chances of an angler like me losing his fly on it, worse still a salmon? And then there is the senselessness of it all. It serves no purpose. What is the point? I beseech you, please, please, please, do not do it!'

He resumed his seat, pleased with the force of his argument, sure he had converted the unconvertible, while his boatman, sitting behind, shook his head forlornly.

The youth was motionless while he considered his response, the scene below and the impassioned plea from the large red-faced fisherman. The tension was palpable, but it did not take long. The youth leaned over the bridge, to ensure that those below could hear him.

'You're a big, fat, ugly English c——t,' he shouted, before bending backwards, scooping up the trolley with both hands, and lobbing it into the river below.

But such things on the riverbank are rare. A day on the river is usually one of harmony, of good humour in joyful places and, just occasionally, triumph against a largely unseen foe. Some say it is all about lunch, the vital punctuation mark in the day's sport. I am not one of them, but nearly.

Lunch here, halfway through the fishing day, was always a time for congregation and reflection, for recounting the adventures of the morning, which pools were fishing best, where were the most seen, what flies did the business, the fly size, what sort of fish were caught, big, small, sea-liced, how did they play, the stories told by the boatmen, the weather, the wind behind or in your face . . . and so on, all to the accompaniment of a gin and tonic, a beer, a warming Amontillado, followed by something more robustly red and soothing from Messrs Berry Bros, then sloe gin, and so the conversation flowed on long into, and beyond, lunch, until those fishing in the afternoon were forced back onto the river at 2.30 p.m., thirty minutes late, still gulping down coffee and chocolates.

My father, long after he had given up fishing, loved coming over here to meet my friends and subject them to an inquisition in his most benign, giggly and distinctly mischievous way. 'Tell me, Mark (the most charming and generous man you could ever meet, and a very good fisherman), what happened this morning, why did you catch nothing when everyone else did?'. Or, 'I hear you lost three this morning, Simon (loves his fishing, has caught masses of fish here and was an old friend of my father), and landed nothing. You are obviously no good.' In short, any shortcoming was mercilessly pounced on by the amiable patriarch, largely for his own benefit and amusement.

There is an annoying Assyrian proverb about days spent fishing not being deducted from man's allotted span, and then Thoreau who, equally irritatingly, wrote, 'Many go fishing . . . without knowing that it is not the fish they are after.' Maybe if it had been 'not just' the fish they are after, for there has to be a chance of catching something, however small.

The joy is the whole package: the river, the boatmen and ghillies, the fishing kit, the weather, the peace and quiet, the beauty, the mental and physical challenge, the occasional triumph, the anticipation and excitement of actually catching something. Even, just now and again, a boy on a bridge with a supermarket trolley. All this with good friends and, of course, lunch.

Always lunch.

Sir Alec

Harold Wilson, by way of a put-down and with reference to his opponent's aristocratic provenance, used to call my Uncle Alec 'the 14th Earl of Home'. It was typical of his gentle manner and irony, never unkind or rude to anyone, that his comeback simply referred to the likelihood that Harold was the 14th Mr Wilson. It is hard to convey his character, not unlike that of his own father, who used to pray audibly as he wandered about the house. In a way Sir Alec was saintlike. Harsh critics will say he could afford to be, but that ignores the breed, for all of them, Alec and his younger siblings, were extraordinarily unmaterialistic and un-grand, when it would have been all too easy to be the opposite. I hope what follows presents something more of his character, perhaps the most unassuming, self-effacing and modest person who ever became foreign secretary and prime minister. A lovely man. I wrote this first in October 2013 after some stellar salmon fishing.

Birgham Dub, the Douglas-Home family beat on the Tweed, had some amazing catches in the first half of last week, both in absolute terms and in relation to others. It was in the same week fifty years ago that 'Sir Alec', as he was affectionately known to all, emerged from a process that he himself later banned, as prime minister. Fanciful, I know, but is it pure coincidence that the pools he loved and fished all his life were so productive, better than any others, exactly fifty years on?

Of course, but how much better if not and it were somehow intended to remind us here in the Borders of a great, a gentle, man, a Borderer and a countryman. I recall driving him over to Douglas in Lanarkshire, somewhat in awe, and asking in the course of that two-hour journey what he thought of Hitler, whom he had met at Munich as Chamberlain's PPS. The reply was short, something along the lines of 'jumped-up little corporal'. Above all, then some thirty years on, he still retained incredulity that an entire nation could have been in thrall to somebody 'so unprepossessing and insignificant', albeit with an undoubted ability to shout at rallies.

Mindful of the effect his words and actions would have on others ('Always think what your actions and what you are saying will do to the other fellow'), he was unfailingly courteous, considered and generous, and with a huge sense of humour and fun. Good at everything – gardening, flower arranging, cricket, shooting, fishing, the *Times* crossword – he was never boastful, with a slightly distracted, otherworldly air about him, amusement and a smile never far from his face.

He could be forgetful; money and passports the most likely to be absent when most needed. It would get him into trouble diplomatically when given something unspeakably awful to eat at a grand dinner on one of his many trips abroad as foreign secretary. He would secrete said sheep's eye (or whatever other horror) in his handkerchief in his pocket when nobody was looking, only to forget he had done so and bring out the handkerchief sometime later to blow his nose, the sheep's eye tumbling onto the floor for all to see.

He was keen on racing, always having a modest flutter on some nag in cahoots with his brother William. A man of simple tastes, moderate in everything, he was never happier than when with his family and friends at home at The Hirsel or Douglas. On days off, he would be mistaken for a scruffy gardener as he emerged from some rhododendron bush.

An avid, almost fervent, BBC weather forecast watcher and listener, he was convinced that the next ice age was about to strike, despite some compelling evidence to the contrary. This is a family failing, determination to overdramatise every weather event, every shower becoming a deluge of biblical proportions, every snowfall a blizzard, every gale a hurricane, and the slightest hint of prolonged sunshine a heatwave and terminal drought.

As was the case with his brothers, his driving was suspect, attention more likely to be on what was over the hedge or fence, be it pigeon, goose, blackcock, covey of partridges, pheasants, you name it, rather than having eyes on the road. I remember sitting on the tailgate of the Land Rover on a day's shooting at Douglas, our legs hanging over the edge as we set off the short distance to the next drive. He went into reverse at speed instead of going forward. We shot towards a stone wall. My fellow tailgater and I yelled, 'Aaaaaagh . . . STOP!!!' – and he did, with inches to spare. I still bear the mental, if not the physical, scars.

He was predictably unreliable in the cartridge-loading department, and it was normal to hear two dull clicks as the first pheasant after lunch came straight over his head, followed by a dismayed 'Oh no, I'm unloaded!', and then mild giggles and cursing from both him and fellow guns.

He wrote a lovely book, a must for all countrymen and women, *Border Reflections*, which shows his prowess at, and love of, fishing. Here are two extracts:

> There was one 38-pounder which took the fly firmly as I let it linger for an extra minute in the wake of a favourite stone, and another 32-pounder which came racing at the fly almost as soon as it touched the surface. The nine fish that morning averaged almost 20 pounds.

If I had to choose between shooting and fishing, I would go for the latter. It is a pursuit which is essentially quiet, and all the beasts and birds will sooner or later come and inspect the fisherman. Such pleasures can of course be enjoyed without a rod, but, with it, every now and again, and sooner than later, the line tightens, and the peace is exchanged for an excitement so tense and tumultuous that every nerve tingles until the prize is won or lost. What more can a man ask of life?

For three years in his late thirties and early forties he lay in bed with TB, a plaster cast encasing his spine, not knowing if he would ever walk, fish or garden again, or be able to resume his political life. It was a terrible time, and the cure, rare in those days, little short of a miracle.

Lord Dunglass, the Earl of Home, Sir Alec Douglas-Home, Lord Home of The Hirsel. His wonderful wife and lifelong companion Elizabeth complained of dizziness and confusion at exactly what her name was at any one time. Prime minister, foreign secretary, MP, Knight of the Thistle, privy councillor, president of the MCC – he was all of these and more.

He was never one to steal anyone's thunder, and so it would not have crossed his mind that the total catch of fifty-eight salmon on his beloved Brigham Dub the first three days of last week was not quite up to the sixty-four salmon he and two friends caught there one February day long ago, but he would never have said it. He was like that. A man of complete integrity, consideration for others and, above all, humour. Right down to the only footwear he wore as he padded around the house, his socks.

A Melancholy Triumph

I have never been capable of unbridled happiness. For some reason for me balance, almost amounting to melancholy, accompanies everything that should be unreservedly joyous. What follows was written some years ago, and more of my friends have joined Martin, James and our little Freddie. Little he was, but would not be now. He would be over thirty and 6 foot 6, just like his brothers. Perhaps that is why I am as I am. It is a selfish true story, of fishing disaster and success, but maybe there is a bit more to it than that. Who knows?

I want you to know how pleased I was, of how the smile refused to leave my normally grumpy exterior for a few hours, and how, after forty-one years of trying, aged fifty-one, I had done it. That annoying monkey was off my back.

The story begins further back, on 19 October 1988. My old friend Martin Wills was staying here but could not fish. Not well enough to wade and the motion of the boat making him dizzy, he was happy to watch. We knew the rain overnight would reach Coldstream and flood the river, but it would take time. The rise started mid-morning and I hurried to the Ledges at the top of the Temple Pool for half an hour before dead sheep would start appearing and all would be hopeless.

Salmon were jumping everywhere, and I instantly hooked one and somehow landed unaided a sea-liced cock fish of 23 pounds.

Time was short. Wading as far as I dared in a waxing river, casting again; instantly the fly was grabbed. It was the last chance to catch another before the full might of the flood hit. Martin, alerted by the commotion of the 23-pounder, had taken up station above me on the bank.

Initially, all was docile, a minute of stalemate with my unseen noble foe, but I was making no impression. It dawned on me that something prodigious was afoot. The fish began to go upstream, into the torrent – a relentless power that I could recall meeting only once before (in Carryweil at Upper Pavilion – but that's another story). And so my quarry set off towards Wark village, despite 6 foot 2 inches of me, my 16-foot Bruce and Walker rod and some 25-pound nylon trying to halt it. As the line and backing poured off the reel, the fish was 150 yards away, upstream, and the backing running out fast. Up to the top of my waders in the torrent and leaning towards the fish, I found everything becoming tighter and tighter until the rod was pointing straight at it, horizontal to the water. *Twang*. The backing snapped. It was over. I never saw my line or the backing again.

I was inconsolable, having just made short shrift of a 23-pounder. In comparison, something extraordinary had happened. Martin had seen it all. 'Epic,' he said. 'You will never forget those ten minutes for as long as you live.' He was right; I never have. Even then, all those years ago, between us, Martin and I had caught more salmon than you have had chicken curries. We agreed we had seen the awesome power of something over, possibly well over, 30 pounds. We considered the possibility that it was foul hooked, with the hook caught in the body of the fish rather than in its mouth, but it had no signs of that, for they usually go downstream and line screams off the reel. This had been unstoppable, slow, relentless power, and directly up and into the oncoming flood.

The brain tumour that prevented Martin fishing, and that he bore so uncomplainingly for years, eventually caused his death, just short of his fortieth birthday. All those lucky to have known him lost a great friend and one of life's true eccentrics. He wore plus fours unbuckled at the knee so that they fell around his ankles, in among his socks; he drove old cars when he could afford new ones; he worked in Bradford as a racing journalist when he did not need to work at all; after hooking a salmon, he would routinely let it run to the bottom of the pool, even into the next one, to increase the chances of it getting off; he used a 15-foot split-cane Hardy's rod, contemptuous of the carbon-fibre brigade. He caught his biggest salmon here on the Temple Pool, with my father rowing him, but would later deny all knowledge of it. He could not countenance his biggest not coming from his beloved Knockando on the Spey.

He had worked out what fishing is all about. It is about excitement, drama, the unpredictable, the thrill, and that things can, will and almost must go wrong. It should never be about catching vast numbers of fish, of bragging about them or showing them off to your friends. That is all transitory pleasure, not real, and gone in a trice. A quick fix, like any other drug, gone in a flash and then you need more. It can never endure.

He was right. All these years later I can still remember that lost monster as if it happened yesterday, but I can recall almost nothing of the others caught since.

With just one exception.

It happened thirteen years later, on 21 October 2001. The river height was much the same, the place identical, in the Ledges, but the river was dropping, not about to flood. I returned from work about 6.15 p.m., with just enough time to have ten minutes in the Ledges, barely a hundred yards from my front door. The fish had been taking badly after incessant small rises; they had been sickened.

After ten casts, in the same place as the epic with Martin, I hooked something. Initially, just as before, nothing much happened, unyielding and solid, stalemate for two or three minutes, and then, with a horrible sense of déjà vu, it set off. Not up this time, but across, and there was nothing I could do to stop it. On and on it went until I saw it splashing by the Wark boat, a hundred yards away. I had burned my fingers on the drum of the reel. I had held the handle tight to stop the reel running, but had to let go as it all went too tight, just short of snapping. Luckily Malcolm had put new backing on the reel (my kit is notoriously rubbish), and all I could see in the gloom was a thin red line stretching out across the river, my 40 yards of Wetcel 2 at the end of it, nowhere to be seen.

My half-functioning brain after ten hours in the office, trying to save tax for the undeserving, registered that something had to be done. Maybe it was foul hooked, and it was getting dark. Make-or-break – literally – time. So I began to haul slowly but steadily and I had to pull really hard to get it back, playing both the fish and the immense power of the river. After another ten minutes, with the light almost totally gone, I had it within twenty-five yards of the bank.

And then I saw its tail, with the nylon coming from the other end, certainly not foul hooked. I shouted, 'S—t, this is f—g huge', hoping that nobody was watching to witness such unseemly behaviour. There was nobody there, no Martin this time, or at least not so far as I could see him.

No gravel, no net, no grassy promontory, nothing; how to land something of that size? After another ten minutes of praying it would not get off (nobody ever really believes you if it does), I had the wallowing monster's head up against the only tuft of grass sticking out from the bank. I dropped the rod, placed my left hand round its tail and my right hand into its mouth with my thumb through its gills. I raced up the bank away from the water, beyond the fence, so it could not escape.

My old friend James, like Martin no longer with us, 'Mr Sponge' in his thank-you letters after staying here, used to tease me with 'They're better dead' when I told him I always put them back nowadays. But I wanted to know if this was over 30 pounds or not and needed to be sure. And so he was. As usual it was a cock fish, well over 31 pounds on the old spring-balance scales – after a while they all weigh heavy, but it was just 30 pounds and 1 ounce on Malcolm's digital scales when he came along to adjudicate. After forty-one years of trying, I had finally caught a 30-pounder, all on my own and in the most testing circumstances. I had joined the exclusive UK 'over-30-pounds club'. Norway, even Russia, is cheating.

Martin was right. I have never forgotten the epic struggle I had lost thirteen years earlier, but now I have a happier memory. Ah yes, that thin line between Kipling's triumph and disaster. Yet, even now, over thirty years later, it is the disaster I remember most. Somehow forged inside my brain is that image of my rod stretching horizontally towards Wark village and the line pouring off the reel as the mighty salmon forged upstream, as if the fly and the line it was attached to did not exist.

I am so lucky to have had such happy and exciting adventures, and to have had them for so long, as compared with both Martin and James, and of course our little Freddie. Maybe he would have liked fishing, maybe he would not. No matter, he should at the very least have had the chance.

Nick's First, and a Duke

When your children are young, you want something special to happen for them. What follows might not seem like much, but a hundred fishermen out of a hundred would not have bothered that afternoon, in blistering sunshine, with a river hardly running and mid-afternoon being the worst possible time. If there is a God, along with that blazing sun, He was looking straight down on Nick.

We were staying with our great friends, Johnny and Fiona Warrender, at Minuntion in Ayrshire, on the upper reaches of the River Stinchar, which runs straight through their land and past the house. It was September 1992. My son Nick was with us, aged not quite seven, his elder brother Richard already at boarding school. We had been invited to fish, but it was hot and the Stinchar was showing its barest bones, so on Saturday morning we played golf at Turnberry.

After lunch, Johnny said that fishing was pretty hopeless but the only pool with any water at all was within walking distance just upstream of the house. If we had nothing better to do, Nick could practise his casting there. The sun was beating down as we strolled across the field, trout rod in hand. The pool was a narrow mini-torrent in the neck and some deepish water for about 10 feet, no more, before it smoothed out into a shallow tail. You could wade across most of the river in wellington boots.

I put a shrimp fly and some 10-pound nylon on the floating line, and briefly showed Nick how to cast into the maelstrom. After a cast or two, and with him placed securely on a rock, I left him to it and retreated a few yards to sit in the sun and absorb the stunning Ayrshire scenery. He continued casting into the white rushing water, briefly letting it come round before casting again. Everything was peace and contentment, with me nearly asleep and my boy happily sploshing his shrimp fly into the water, over and over again.

'Daddy, I think I have got one on,' I heard dimly from my semi-comatose state.

Not budging, I said, 'Don't be silly. You have caught the bottom.'

'No, Daddy, I have got one on.'

Finally stirring onto my feet, I stood next to him on his rock. The rod was not bent, but there was no sign of the line, other than it pointing straight into the deep hole just below the white water. I took the rod and lifted it, increasing the strain and whatever was on the end moved – not, it would seem, the bottom.

'You really have got one on!' I said, giving the rod back to him and going to get the all-too-small net, which luckily we had brought with us. There was insufficient water for the salmon to run out of the pool, so with Nick hanging on, it cruised around and around in the deep hole, into the whirlpool and then out again. As it tired, I moved away from Nick's side. Up until then I had been hanging onto him to make sure he did not follow the fish into the deep hole. I directed him to bend the rod more and try to bring it closer, as the fish tired.

Eventually he did, no mean feat for a six-year-old, and I had it, head first into the net, a red cock fish of 9 pounds, hooked, played and landed by my little boy in impossible conditions. The shrimp fly was securely in its scissors. We kept it, partly because nobody would have believed us, and took it back to the house, to astonished and gleeful greetings all round. The photograph still sits in full view here at home, Nick proudly sitting next to his defeated quarry, holding the rod, with an equally young Jack Warrender sitting behind.

The Duke of Wellington came to lunch the next day, after fishing half-heartedly at Knockdolian the day before, conditions hopeless, he reflected.

'I caught one,' said Nick, to the warmest possible ducal congratulations and surprise.

Expert fisherman duke, or six-year-old novice, we are all the same to the fish. That is as it should be.

Red-Letter Days

Torn between wanting to make the most of it when things are good, and not being entirely comfortable with numbers for their own sake, I am fatally conflicted. For some reason, numbers do matter, they fascinate, they grab the headlines. I suspect for all the wrong reasons.

When I was a boy, in the days before they reared pheasants in the Newmarket area, my father was one of six guns who shot over a thousand wild pheasants at Stetchworth on each of two days. With his host, on the day in between the two big days, the two of them shot 250 by 'doing a few hedgerows'. Few would dispute that these were red-letter days, especially as there was not a reared pheasant among them, but I would bet you that even shortly after such a bonanza, my father would have struggled to recall any single bird he had shot.

By contrast, on a day's shooting when the total bag is forty, and you shoot say five of those, you can remember every one, especially if one or two are 'screamers'. I gave up shooting nearly forty years ago, but oddly can still remember some of the (very few) stratospheric pheasants I did shoot. That is the curious thing about what we call 'red-letter days', normally meaning big numbers. You cannot remember any one incident in the whole day; it is a blur of activity and action.

So it is with fishing.

For most of my life I have lived within a gnat's crochet of the Tweed. It has been the most productive salmon river in the UK. It still is today. Before you or other fishing persons say it, I have been lucky and spoiled. No argument. The result is that there have been a few 'red-letter days', possibly more than I think, as the definition, the hurdle to be jumped, inevitably rises the more there are, the very definition of being spoiled. At the time, all these days were great, with me catching loads of fish, payback for all those interminable times when they would not take, or weren't even there, or we were blown off by gales, wrecked by floods, beaten by blazing sun and drought . . . and so on.

Now, in retrospect, writing about them, or thinking of doing so, I cannot escape a feeling of guilt. Was it too easy? What was the point?

I will not bore you with the list, but on inspection of the detail, I can report that most of those days were 'red-letter' just because they were not too easy. Indeed, for some, I fool myself that nobody else would have caught them, or not have caught so many.

The Temple Pool here is my favourite. When the river is low, it is flat, a hundred yards wide, with barely any current. Most anglers would take one look and go elsewhere. But that is when I like it, and for those who know, it can be waded. There is a concrete wall behind you, so where do you land the fish when you are on your own, as I always am? It is all part of the challenge. It has to be difficult, or there is no point. I keep the Temple Pool for myself on Saturdays, but seldom use it when it is a perfect height, somewhere between 1 foot 6 inches and 2 foot 3 inches, because then the tenants will want to be there.

It was Saturday, 21 October 2003; the height was minus one inch. The river had been low for weeks, the beats below Coldstream cleaning up, but the fish could just get here, or at least some of them. Minus one inch on our gauge is incredibly low, more than a foot under what we normally class as summer level. It rained all that day and there was a strong wind from the northeast, but the

Temple was sheltered, the water flat calm. I had an inkling that I would be in business. The previous evening, after work I had briefly waded the Ledges at the top of the Temple and my fishing book says, 'Caught 2, 7 and 6 pounds, size-10 Ally shrimp, floating line, 3 more "follows".' Those three had followed it as I hand-lined the fly round, the wakes all too visible in the flat calm water.

The water temperature was 41°F, cold, and I caught eight the next morning, on a floater; all were released. With boatman Malcolm's guidance, one of our brave tenants waded it in the afternoon, and caught another five, making thirteen for the day, when most would never have looked at it. The exciting thing is the 'follows': the bow wave coming after the fly. They come after it for what seems like ages. Will they take it, or won't they? Rule of thumb, the longer the 'follow', the less likely they will actually take it, but you never quite know. You have to go on handlining at the same speed. I shouted at some of them, 'Take it!' That did no good.

No fluke, I have repeated it several times since, catching eight or nine in a day – and one day even ten – in similarly unpromising conditions in the Temple Pool. Because of the vertical wall, you cannot land them and I carry no net. When played out, I cradle them in my arms, kneeling in the water, and gently extract the hook, and away they swim. There have been disasters, but too few to mention.

There have been bigger days in easier water, but they do not cut it in the essential difficulty stakes. I prefer pools in the most marginal conditions. I can afford to, for I am spoiled.

But now I am not so sure. Is the difficulty alone enough justification for catching so many? Caught on a fly? Tick. In the most challenging conditions? Tick. On my own, no help? Tick. But does it meet the standard, the gold standard, by which we should all review our conduct? From Luke Jennings' wonderful book *Blood Knots* – a memoir of fishing and of his friendship with Robert Nairac, the British Army intelligence officer murdered by the Provisional IRA:

> I understand now why Robert was absolutist in his method, and why he spoke of honour and dry fly in the same sentence. Because the rules we impose on ourselves are everything, especially in the face of nature. It's not a question of wilfully making things harder, but of a purity of approach without which success has no meaning. And this, ultimately, was his lesson: that the fiercest joy is to be a spectator of your own conduct and find no cause for complaint.

If I can equate the 'honour' of dry-fly fishing for trout with the 'honour' of fly fishing for salmon, I think I can pass my own test, measured by my own standards. However, that fascination for high scores still remains to some extent. Will I have any more of the 'red-letter days' that litter the entries in my fishing book? I very much doubt it, for after catching two, three or four, I shall go home. Perhaps, after all, I am lurching erratically towards Robert's 'fiercest joy' and finding 'no cause for complaint'.

I hope so.

A Good Frost and Puppsie

In our ever warming world, it is easy to forget that salmon dislike heat. If I were to obsess about anything, it is that we have not done enough to reduce the future peak water temperatures in our rivers. What follows is just one example of how obvious it is that, despite that old film title *Some Like It Hot*, our salmon most definitely do not.

Our Lancashire Heeler, Puppsie, so called because, like her owner, she has never grown up, has been outside in the garden all day, enjoying the Sabbath sunshine. It is unseasonably warm, the air coming from the tropics, high humidity on a tepid sou'wester. It arrived on Saturday with cloud, a marked change to the cool nights that had dominated until then. Puppsie had spent the first half of the week inside. Until then, the fishing had been good.

You may recall, or even own, one of those absurd watches that predict if you will catch a fish based on barometric pressure. It was and is tosh. The same could never be said of Puppsie. She is an utterly dependable indicator of outside weather conditions and thus of the likelihood of success with rod and line.

I have noticed, born of years observing the habits of our autumn fish, that heat and humidity are not good. You might catch something, but not much. By the opposite token, cold nights, preferably frost and a cooling northerly are the business, in spades.

Not only are salmon more comfortable in the cold, they go far north to feed in the ocean after all, but the sudden onset of cold in the autumn seems to trigger aggressive behaviour. The cock salmon in particular attack your fly with uncontrolled forcefulness.

I first noticed this on 15 September 1969 at Upper Pavilion. It had been warm for many days, the river lowish, with fish about but they would not take. The night of 14–15 September was cold with a sharp frost, not something you will ever see in mid-September fifty years later. Puppsie would not have been outside on that bitter morning. On my gap year, my father went off to St Boswells Mart to sell lambs. I had the river to myself. I cannot recall expecting much, as the river was still low and I had not spotted the temperature thing. We had caught nothing for two weeks beforehand.

I started in the Brigend, just by where I parked my Mini Traveller motor car, with a floating line and a small Blue Charm. I caught eight before it fell apart, then another three on a Hairy Mary – eleven in all in the Brigend, all between 5 and 7 pounds. By then it was well into the afternoon, so upstream to Carryweil where one more fell to the Hairy Mary, before it too collapsed, when a Jeannie was employed to catch another in Carryweil, before getting the last one in the Kingswellees. In total fourteen salmon or grilse after two weeks of near blanks. My father was surprised when he returned from the Mart. I lost none, with just four other pulls. An astonishing day, all the better for the lack of anticipation. I am still haunted by the probability that I might not have bothered, so poor was the prognosis.

As a control test it was perfect. The only thing that had changed was the frost and the consequent drop in both air and water temperature. My father defeated me the following day as it became colder still. I stuck with a floater and caught two, while his superior *savoir faire* persuaded him to go with a sinker. He was right; he caught five.

Until this humid and muggy weather passes, do not bust a gut on the river. Puppsie is even now outside all day. I will let you know when she stays inside.

That is the time to go fishing.

Don't Get Me Started

There is something excoriatingly annoying about the Great British Public's obsession with animals and birds that look pretty or noble but do untold damage to those below them in the food chain or to other parts of the ecosystem. The careful exercise of balance and control is essential if we are to ensure that these prey species are not obliterated by those at the top of the chain, which it has been decreed should be protected by the Wildlife and Countryside Act of 1981. There is also an element of class warfare in the mix, as well as a kind of romanticism and anthropomorphism encouraged by some TV naturalists, which makes it more complicated. Here are just a few examples of where it already has, or shortly will, go horribly wrong.

I am writing this after seeing some shocking pictures of the tree damage now being done by beavers on Tayside. If nothing is done to control them, it will become accepted as the norm. The GBP think they are cute and everyone wants to reintroduce them everywhere to solve our eco woes.

I have never understood why so many people think a small animal is capable of undoing all the ills we humans have wrought on the environment. Do they really stop flooding? The only property-damaging, life-threatening floods on the Tweed are those exceeding 10 feet down here at Coldstream; below that they are routine and do little harm. And when you see the Tweed in a 14–17-foot flood, as I have several times since coming here, it is frankly laughable that a puny beaver dam could have any beneficial effect at all on that massive surging torrent of water. Except, of course, that the debris from the dam will end up either down here or in the sea.

153

While the beavers' beneficial effects are debatable here, their negative effects are not: farmers' fields are flooded because beavers have burrowed into and destroyed flood banks; they destroy our valuable and much-needed riparian trees, which governments are encouraging us to plant; and they then block tributaries with their dams. The Tweed is one of the best salmon rivers because of its extensive spawning streams, stretching to thousands of kilometres across the south and east of Scotland, even into northern England. As the global climate in the UK lurches between extreme drought and flood, it is becoming increasingly common for many, perhaps most, of these streams to be very low flowing in the autumn, the crucial time for migratory salmon and trout to move upstream. That makes the free passage of fish hard enough already, even without the streams being blocked by beaver dams; when they are dammed, it becomes impossible. The Tweed Commission has the statutory power to knock down natural obstructions to migration, and will have to exercise that power in order to allow our adult migrating fish to get to their spawning grounds. This will have to be done at great expense every year, as beavers rebuild their dams as soon as possible after they have been removed. Taking that into account, their impact on flooding on a large river such as the Tweed will be completely insignificant.

The destruction beavers can cause in a highly populated and managed landscape appears to be ignored by all those in favour. Ten years ago, the River Tweed Commission chief executive Nick Yonge and I went to see the SNP's Scottish Environment Minister, Mike Russell. Our mission was to dissuade him from allowing the reintroduction of beavers. Despite our passionately expressed arguments, he was utterly determined to bring them back, regardless of our valid concerns. Just a few beavers on the Tay can wreak the devastation outlined above. Now extrapolate twenty years forward to a time when there are thousands of beavers throughout the UK and you might begin to see why Nick and I went on a mission to try to stop it.

In reality, that number could be much higher. Experience shows that beaver populations increase by about 16 per cent a year – a small amount when numbers are low, but this becomes a massive increase as the population grows. Around a hundred years ago, Latvia and Lithuania – countries similar in size to Wales – reintroduced just a few individual beavers. Both now have beaver populations of around 100,000. At least hunting them is allowed there as a management tool, which keeps numbers under control, but would such management tools ever be allowed in the UK? I very much doubt it. And yet adverse human–beaver interactions will be far greater here, where our human population of 65 million far outnumbers the 3.5 million of the Baltic states.

The lament of people like me is that uncontrolled reintroductions and protections, without thought as to what will happen when the species introduced or protected becomes the problem, is just plain stupid. We now have no hedgehogs here, and we have badgers galore. There has been no change in farming practices, the oft-given reason for the hedgehogs' demise, for we live in an area covered by a woodland. Forty years ago we had hedgehogs everywhere here, and very few badgers. Now we have badgers coming out of our ears, and not a hedgehog in sight. None. The badgers have killed all the hedgehogs. No argument. They also dig up all our bumble-bee nests.

Many years ago, under licence, a goosander was shot here and disgorged the contents of its last meal. There were six young salmon, two young trout and a tiny eel. Just one meal for one goosander on one day out of 365 days a year. We have over a thousand goosanders on the Tweed catchment and, in the winter, flocks of cormorants, bigger birds with larger appetites. Hundreds of thousands of our young fish are eaten every year by these birds. Yet the salmon is increasingly endangered where goosanders and cormorants are distinctly not. They have few, if any, natural predators, so their numbers can grow unchecked, as does the damage they wreak on vulnerable prey species. The GBP is ignorant of the underwater slaughter going on day in day out, yet there are howls of protest at the thought of anyone trying to control, i.e. kill, just some of the perpetrators of this carnage, the birds.

In June, some years ago, my brother Simon kindly invited me on a trip to the Farne Islands to see the nesting guillemots, puffins, kittiwakes and terns (common, Arctic and sandwich), among many others. Before landing, the skipper took us to an Outer Farne to look at the grey seals, of which there are many thousands, in increasing numbers, around the shores of the UK. The party on the boat was mixed, the majority cooing and aahing at the sight of these huge animals lying on the rocks. Every member of my brother's party was thinking instead of the gauntlet the salmon migrating to the Tweed, working their way up the Northumbrian coast, would have to run to get through to Berwick harbour and comparative safety. Apart from humans, only killer whales, orcas, can control seal numbers. I long ago accepted that the GBP will not countenance the killing of seals, but does the GBP give one single thought to the uncontrolled increase in their numbers and the consequences for the prey species they eat? No, not one. Of course, it was right to protect our grey seals when their numbers dropped to 500 – but now that they exceed 120,000 and are still increasing, has anyone got a plan to protect the species that they eat? I thought not.

Underneath it all is a class issue. There are those who think that anyone who wants to kill or control anything is an upper-class tweedy dolt – 'the nasty brigade' as Mr Packham called them in 2016 – and accordingly they are seen as politically unacceptable and safe to ignore as worthless. It gets to a point where tweedy dolts like me can no longer watch *Springwatch* or *Autumnwatch* or whatever other 'watch' is on the TV, because the presenters seem reluctant to acknowledge, for example, the huge damage inflicted by predators on our smaller and most vulnerable songbirds, waders and fish.

I hope Mary Colwell will not mind me mentioning her here, for what is desperately needed is balance and dialogue. She has written a beautiful book, *Curlew Moon*, about the disastrous shrinkage in the numbers of that most evocative of birds. Whereas predation is far from the whole reason for the decline in curlew numbers, it is part of the picture. She has now tackled the whole question of predation and balance in another book, *Beak, Tooth and Claw*, trying to seek common ground between the two warring sides. I wish her well.

To say that those atop the food chain, the predators, should never be controlled, even when they are threatening the very existence of what they eat, is absurd. Even more shameful are those who would shoot every goosander, cormorant, hen harrier and sparrow hawk.

We need dialogue and balance. At present the laissez-faire 'you mustn't control anything' brigade have the ascendance. That cannot go on because those unseen millions of little (and big) birds, little (and bigger) fish, little (and big) hedgehogs, and trees (both big and little) are paying the price.

Does It Matter?

Somehow weights of the larger salmon we catch matter much more than the weights of the smaller fish, a considerable difficulty in these days of over 90 per cent catch and release. Typically, accountants like me think there is no point in recording something unless it is accurate. The bigger the fish, the greater the inaccuracies, because we anglers see so few of them. But then it is only the big ones whose precise weights are important to us. 'My biggest salmon was . . .' goes the oft-heard refrain, or something similar. Figures seem to matter at the big end of the salmon scale, even when they are wrong. Or do they?

I was rowing my younger son Nick in the Temple Pool when he hooked something that he initially thought 'really quite tiny'. About ten minutes later it came to the surface for the first time, in full view of us in the boat. I cannot remember what I said, but it was not repeatable. To net a fish securely, you must get the head in first. I could not remove the hook without hauling it on board (the boat was tied to the Temple wall where you cannot get out). It was all I could do to lift it out of the net and into the boat, and then I really struggled to lift it back into the water and hold it there until it was fit enough to swim away. What did it weigh? I have no idea except that it was big, not that long (about 40 inches), but incredibly thick, and we know that so much of the weight is in the girth.

We put it in the fishing book at 25 pounds, but I am troubled that Nick has been done out of a 30-pounder. I keep looking at the cast of my really dead and weighed 30-pounder and mentally compare it to Nick's. His would be very close to 30 pounds, closer than my 25-pound estimate would suggest. Most inexperienced anglers tend to overestimate by some margin, because they never see, or have seen, big fish, and they get carried away.

Estimates are not always on the generous side. I am reminded of another incident when accuracy was not an option.

Ghillie Paul Hume was rowing one of our tenant's guests, Henry Lax, in our Cauld stream. It was early November 2012. They hooked what was clearly a very big fish, and after a struggle they netted it from one of the croys* on the south side. Paul's measuring tape said it was 49 inches long. Big, seriously big.

Laudably and sensibly, the advice from Henry Lax, when asked by Paul if he wanted to keep it to find out for sure how much it weighed, was that he had caught bigger fish in Norway, so would be happy to release it unharmed. And so it was released, accurately measured but unweighed.

The Tweed standard length–weight chart goes up to only 48 inches, or 42.8 pounds. Mr Lax's monster was a full inch longer. After much discussion, the consensus was to put it in the book at 35 pounds in order to err on the safe side. It was also not the thickest fish in terms of girth, but even so, at 49 inches, it was huge. Paul says he has only once seen a salmon that size before, when working on the nets. That one was weighed at 45 pounds. Paul's view is that this one was also over 40 pounds.

But our records will never show that. Does it matter in these days of catch and release that the weights of really big fish will seldom be completely accurate? Even with weigh nets, trying to hold the net up and steady to read an accurate weight with the huge fish still alive and thrashing around is almost guaranteed to result in an inaccurate reading.

---

* A barrier built out in a stream as a fish shelter or means of allaying bank erosion.

If it matters to you, there is no real option other than to kill the fish to be able to weigh it properly. Most anglers will not do that, so it cannot matter that much. But it will mean that another Domesday Book of big fish may never happen, for the weights will be unreliable and there will be no photographs of the very dead monsters.

No matter. Times move on.

A November Splash?

Something very odd happened in 2014. The Tweed's famed and fabled autumn run stopped coming. In November 2013 we caught 230 mainly bright silver salmon here at the Lees. Since then the successive November scores here have been 45, 34, 33, 14, 3, 3 and 4. In other words, we have caught about half the November 2013 catch spread over the following seven years. The whole-river November catch in 2019 was 130 salmon, not much more than half what we caught on our two miles of river in 2013. The whole-river November catch in November 2013 was 4,578, a small matter of 4,448 higher than its equivalent seven years later. Don't blame fishing conditions; Novembers have always been fickle weather-wise, and recent ones no more fickle than those pre-2014.

Not long ago I used to walk along the banks of the Temple Pool in November with salmon jumping everywhere, two or three in the air at the same time. Now I am surprised if I see a splash. Even if I do, I will suspect it is an early descending kelt, having done its spawning business and making a backwards run for the sea.

Some say they saw it coming, or at least they say that now. Trust me, they did not. Yes, there was a general trend towards more summer salmon, but it had been gradual. Oddest of all, the children of the massive record Tweed catch of 2010 – 23,219 salmon – should have been those coming back in 2014. More eggs must have been deposited in the winter of 2010–11 than any other year in living memory, yet the 2014 total catch was 7,767, a third of the parent-generation catch. How could that possibly happen?

By a process of elimination, we can rule out what did not cause it, but that leaves us with only conjecture as to the precise reason. Whatever it was, it was cataclysmic. It was not in the river, for there was no exceptional in-river event that could have caused such devastation between 2011 and 2012–13, when most of the 2010-run offspring would have left the river. Some say that when there are too many adults fighting over a small area of spawning ground, it can be counterproductive, as existing nests of eggs can be disturbed by others being created in the same place, the so-called 'overcutting of the redds'. It was an argument the netting fraternity used to excess from the 1960s to 1980s to justify the vast tonnages of salmon they caught and killed. On enquiry, nobody has ever seen this 'overcutting' process in action, and even if it happens (one overcrowded spawning salmon fighting with and muscling in on another), it is impossible to see how it can be counterproductive. It might do no good, because the spawning space is filled anyway, but to produce fewer juveniles? Really? And anyone who says that birds, our goosanders and cormorants, could have caused this collapse is just plain wrong. Of course they kill young fish, but with so many more produced from the massive 2010 run, they should have made even less of an impact on surviving smolt numbers.

This is where everyone, scientists especially, comes unstuck. There has never been a convincing argument to explain that sudden and massive collapse of fresh-running salmon in the autumns since 2014. As the best autumn river, the Tweed was most adversely affected, but all other rivers with late runs of salmon have noticed exactly the same. All of which points to some event in the only medium common to fish in all Scottish rivers: the sea.

What I can understand is that once the autumn fish stop coming, nature will allow some other cohort to take its place. Pre-2014, any spring or summer salmon eggs would hatch but would have to compete with so many millions more autumn-run eggs in the same limited space. Inevitably the autumn-run eggs and offspring would dominate. But what happens if the autumn salmon stop coming? The eggs of the spring and summer fish suddenly have the playing field to themselves, with no competition, more food and the chances of survival massively improved. You are bound to end up with more spring and summer fish. Suddenly, the few remaining late-running autumn salmon are at a disadvantage, and it is they that will now struggle to survive against the far greater numbers of the offspring of the earlier arrivers. It is logical that once the dominance is broken, those who were second and third will go on gathering strength. In short, we are going to end up with spring and summer salmon being by far in the ascendant, and the autumn run very much an afterthought, coming in last in every sense. Curiously, exactly what happened a hundred years ago between 1905 and 1925. It then remained an early-running, mainly spring river for the next fifty years.

My father said this would happen. Don't you just hate it when your parents are right? He could be liberal with his interpretation of how long it would take – I heard him say anything between thirty and seventy years – but he knew it would change, even if the marine mechanisms for such dramatic shifts were a mystery, as they still are to us. Speculations about sea-surface temperatures, changing ocean currents and consequent movements in food sources and competition from other fish, especially from mackerel, abound. But it is undeniably odd that one section of our salmon populations can prosper at the same time as another falls off the proverbial cliff.

Does it matter that we cannot work out why it happens? The scientists don't like it, for they tell me that knowledge is everything. But sometimes there are no clear answers or solutions. Having damaged the rivers with pollution, obstructions and overfishing, it was thought that we could correct our mistakes with hatcheries. Did that do the salmon any good? Have we been able to halt the Atlantic salmon's recently accelerated retreat to a comparatively few rivers in the very north of their former range? Has the devastation on Scottish west-coast rivers stopped? No. So one might ask whether there is any point in having precise knowledge of how these dramatic shifts happen if there is nothing, but nothing, you can do about it in the vastness of the North Atlantic ocean.

There is something ironic about the fact that the Atlantic salmon was at its strongest between the 1920s and 1960s, before anybody thought of the advanced river-management practices of today and despite massive pollution, huge human predation (netting and rods), blocked tributaries, and a number of other ills, and with river boards run by one man and his dog from a solicitor's office somewhere (on the Tweed, it was in Jedburgh), and with a lot of bailiffs and a part-time clerk – but not a scientist in sight. If this reads as a denigration of science and scientists, you misread my point entirely; for within river systems, which to an extent we can influence and control, the collection of data upon which we can base our actions is a crucial tool to ensure our rivers are as productive, as much of a stronghold, for our fish as possible.

However, so far as these mysterious cycles and macro movements in the oceans are concerned, you could argue we have no option but to let them happen and marvel that nature can, indeed must, do its own thing without our own, often malign, human intervention. If the cycle theorists, my father among them, are right, I will never again see the Tweed alive with fresh salmon in November and, if it takes another sixty years, nor will most of you. Instead, I might well see the Temple Pool heaving with beautiful fresh spring salmon in April and May, just as I did in the 1960s.

'Might well see' are the operative words, for the jury is still out. The smart money is that something totally new, with no historical precedent, is happening, and that the many effects of global warming are making life challenging for our salmon, to say the least. If so, reliance on historical cycles and the idea that 'it has happened before, it will come right again naturally given time' may be far too optimistic.

Which in turn might mean that the abundances of salmon that we saw 'when I was but a lad' will never happen again, or at least not until global warming is both stopped and reversed.

It is a sobering thought, but for now our job is to keep things going for our salmon as best we can. The Tweed needs to be a stronghold, a safe haven for those travellers that make it back here.

A Switlyk and the PC Police

I might be hopeless at all things techy, but even I have spotted that, among all the obvious benefits of social media, the downside is that what you assume to be a harmless post can make you a global hate figure before you can say 'iPhone'. I have never understood why those who use it so exhaustively, posting pictures of their every waking moment, broadcasting to friends and strangers alike, should think the rest of us are remotely interested. Ms Switlyk, global huntress, discovered its perils the hard way, but it could happen to any of us.

So there you are, on your own, about to land a very large cock salmon after an epic fight, when your thoughts inevitably turn to 'What am I going to do with it?' You beach it, and find the fly well down its throat. Not sure you can save it anyway, and fancying a bit of smoked salmon, you knock it on the head, as you were perfectly legally, post 1 July on the Tweed, entitled to do. Back to the hut, congratulations all round and next thing a photo of a clearly dead 20-pound sea-liced cock salmon is on Instagram.

Cue vitriol, the first response being, 'That fish looks dead . . .', followed by many more, nothing like so polite. The result? The picture of the 20-pound salmon was removed from Instagram for fear of global infamy for the innocent captor. Welcome to today's world.

What would you have done?

We all have our own views, but mine is that I would never have killed it, long ago having decided that killing any salmon when there are so few makes no sense. I enjoy seeing them swim away. But the lucky fisherman with his 20-pounder had done nothing (legally) wrong, except post it on Instagram. In other words, if you ever kill a salmon nowadays, take it home, put it in the freezer, smoke it, but don't tell anyone.

Ask Larysa Switlyk, the exotically named American huntress, who shot a wild sheep on Islay. She posted a smiling selfie with her rifle and the very dead sheep. There were thousands of quasi-nuclear explosions on social media; it was headlines on the BBC news. I am told some of those sheep, just like red-deer stags, have to be culled every year. She had done nothing wrong, except . . .

If you kill some fish or animal, regardless of how justified or not it is, or you want to show off your picture of your first 30-pound salmon, please don't. I have photos of rows of salmon caught and killed by our fishing guests in the 1980s, best now shredded for fear of discovery and some belated witch hunt. The increasingly urbanised British public simply cannot take the reality of death in nature, especially if humans have had any hand in it.

Keep it quiet. No pictures. It is the only way.

Lanrick

There is a hidden joy of a river at the top of the Forth estuary, known to few, almost as if those who do know do not want anyone else in on their little secret. You drive from Edinburgh to Stirling, then hang a left past the Blair Drummond Safari Park, left again before Doune and you are there, at Lanrick.

There was a castle there, but my old friend Aly Dickson took it on himself, and a digger, to knock it down. Lanrick Castle was listed, even if it was pretty hideous, so the authorities took a dim view, believing that you could not let any old Tom, Dick or Aly destroy something just because they disliked it. But Aly was right. It was dangerous and crumbling, a magnet to local kids despite the fencing to keep them out, and nobody would give any money to make it good. Aly found himself before the beak with a good deal of finger-wagging and tut-tutting. He was fined £1,000 and told never ever to do it again. Which of course, he could not, as he already had.

His castle remains below ground, under a neatly formed mound, beside the lovely Castle Flats Pool, by the glorious fishing hut and where Aly's and Penny's adored son Sandy, who very tragically died when far too young, is remembered so beautifully. This is all beside one of the prettiest and most exciting rivers you will ever see, the one you have never heard of, the River Teith. I just love going there for a day's fishing, and feel so lucky to be invited.

I am not sure why, but if you offered me just one more day's fishing anywhere, it might well be on the Teith at Lanrick. It is not just that the river itself, and its surrounds, are dreamy. The whole day is one of unalloyed happiness, and of being perfectly looked after, lunch seemingly appearing from nowhere but always the perfect mixture of food, fun and a certain amount of drink. The hut is magnificent, indeed the word 'hut' being wholly misleading; 'palace' might be more accurate. I could look at the views both up and down the river, with the glorious trees and mountains as backdrop, forever. Indeed, despite my obvious affection for the noble art and the likelihood of piscatorial success in those lovely pools, there is nowhere I find it harder to drag myself out of and back to business after lunch.

Aly is one of my oldest friends, wholly responsible for introducing me to the game of golf. When we were all trying to earn a crust in our early twenties in London, Aly and his parents let me come and stay in their house at Barrow, just outside Bury St Edmunds in Suffolk, more frequently than they probably would have liked. Aly's mother Sheila had been a scratch golfer, had won many tournaments and simply could not understand why we ordinary mortals found the game so mystifyingly difficult. She used to smile benignly and say things like 'You just line it up, take a swing and hit it there.'

Well, of course, how silly of me! Aly was a member at Royal Worlington, just a few miles away from Barrow, reputed to be (it is) one of the best 9-hole courses in the land. I recall seeing that legendary (for England) golfer (and cricketer), Leonard Crawley wandering around with his dogs. Thankfully, he was spared observation of my swing, as we were playing some way behind.

At much the same time that I legged it from London to the Scottish Borders in the late 1970s, Aly did something similar, moving to his mother's Scottish family (Stroyan) home at Lanrick and has been there ever since. Among his many talents he is a superb builder, an interior designer and, latterly, an excellent potter. He has built and extended his own house, and has built beautiful houses for his mother and sister, and paying fishing guests can rent the most comfortable bothy extension to his own house. For somewhere so accessible from Glasgow and Edinburgh and with immediate access to at least two motorways, its seclusion and quietness are surprisingly complete.

I cannot recall ever going there to fish without some fishy contact or success. The pools are all lovely, varied, and you feel you are going to catch one with every cast. Unlike my beloved Tweed, it is a manageable size, all easily wade-able, and every yard of those sparkling pools is a delight. I am blessed to have been there so often. They tell me that you will catch more further downstream at Blair Drummond, which has bigger holding pools. So be it. Given the choice, you will find me in the Gravel Bank or in the Dam, or, my favourite, Sandy's Pool, at Lanrick, sometime in the early autumn.

Every time.

Simply Magnificent

Although, at the age of seventy-one, I love my fishing, there is one aspect that haunts me. I do not want to damage the salmon I catch and jeopardise their prospects of getting to the spawning beds. They are only passing through, fleeting visitors as they seek to complete their (usually) ultimate journey. It is a privilege to have them swimming within a hundred yards of where I live, all the way from Greenland. I never kill them, but occasionally one dies from being fatally hooked down its throat. When it does, I scream and howl with anguish. They are beautiful, noble and strong fish. I know my attitude is full of contradictions, so don't bother telling me. This is one short story where my friend, the fish I had just caught, swam away safely. So beautiful was he, I could hardly have borne it had he not.

I have no idea exactly what it weighed. Momentarily lying prone, on its side but in the water, after the drama with the hook, it was precisely three lengths of my size-13 boots. Laying my rod alongside, the rod butt end opposite the inner V of its tail, I scratched a mark on the rod by the tip of its nose. I would measure it more accurately when I got home. It was one of the most magnificent creatures you will ever see.

It all started with a vague notion of going out, late one evening, for half an hour with a small fly and a sink tip.* I was fed up with the pernicious cold and those heavy sinking lines, such hard work, but with water now over 40°F, might they come up to something nearer the surface? The wind was nagging but it was more southerly than those vicious easterlies. The line shot out, so nice to fish with

---

* A sink tip combines a sinking and floating line.

a lighter line, even if the salmon are still lurking near the bottom. The date was 9 April 2013, the height 1 foot 7 inches and the water exactly 40°F. It was also my first proper sortie of 2013, early enough for someone who dislikes cold.

In the Glide pool it is smooth, but wasn't that a swirl where my fly was in the water? Everything had stopped and had gone, well, solid. You know when you hook something big. I pulled but nothing gave; it pulled and I had to let it go, driven by solid impulse and power into the deep water and towards the other bank, seventy yards away. I knew I would win in the end so long as the hook and my nylon held. It had been on the rod since October, the last time I had used that sinking-tip line.

After twenty minutes, it was starting to wallow, getting closer and, like any true heavyweight, once over on its side, you have it as it struggles to become upright. Then triumph quickly turns to concern, for there is no sign of the fly; it must be in its throat. What to do? Cut the line and leave the fly there, or risk taking it out from where I could now see it lodged, well back in the throat with one hook in the top of the gill ribs? One slip as I try to take it out, and the jugular will be punctured, game over for the fish. But if I leave the fly there, will it survive the six months until it spawns in October? Forceps in hand, I decided to take the hook out. So, into the mouth, grasp the fly, twist gently to extract it. I had it, but any blood? As its heart pumps, the water will go red; you curse and accept the inevitable. But my magnificent friend and I got lucky. There was no blood.

I measured it – no camera, as usual I had left my mobile behind – and finally I knelt with him in the water. He was ready to go. 'Him?' I hear you cry. Trust me, he was a boy, his head being all male and the whole shape. I know it is more difficult to tell in the spring, but I have no doubt. If he had died, I would have cursed and yelled; a seal had already had a go at the underside of the tail, so thick I could hardly get my hand round it, and another seal swipe had left a white mark on his back. He was magnificent, and as he slowly swam away he looked fantastic.

What did he weigh? Both measurements, my size-13 boots and the mark on the rod, came out at 39 inches and, unlike an autumn fish, he was all muscle, no flab, liced and straight from the sea. In his prime. Was he 25 pounds? No. Was he 20 pounds? Yes, easily. The immediate thought in my mind was 23 or 24 pounds, and the chart said 24 pounds. Does it matter? No, for he gave me half an hour of my fishing life that I will never forget. I have caught bigger fish in the autumn, but never in the spring. Others have caught bigger springers, but not many.

A Very Fishy Pandemic

If Covid-19 has taught us anything, it is how powerless we are in the face of a new and unknown disease. It is the same in the animal world, although it is even worse for other living things because their ills cannot be prioritised as human diseases are and, of course, they do not sense that isolation, or keeping apart, is a big part of the answer. Animals and fish form packs and shoals for safety against predation – exactly the behaviour that plays into any new infectious disease's hands. I hope never to see repeated the devastation I saw in the spring of 1967 caused by ulcerative dermal necrosis (UDN). I wrote this piece in 2013 when, thankfully for only a very brief period, it looked like recurring.

Disease has appeared in the last week or two. It is distressing to see, especially in the Tweed's comparatively weak spring salmon stocks. The unusual element is its timing, coming when water temperatures are rising. Instinctive reactions are that this could be the same as the UDN of the late 1960s. That initial 1967 outbreak came in very cold water; it began to disappear and fish healed up and recovered as water temperatures rose. Unnervingly, just as in 1967, catches here have declined as more and more fish have become infected.

The cause of UDN has never been discovered, and therefore nothing can be done to stop it. The white fungus on affected fish is the result of the disease, the fungus growing when the skin is broken by the infection raging. If unchecked, the fungus will grow all over the fish's body, starting with the head and then working down its back. At this point, the fish is feeling very ill, typically wallowing near or even slightly above the surface of the water. In 1967, to spare their agonies, we netted them out of the water before they died, dispatched them humanely and buried them in lime pits. Thousands died. I remember looking over Kelso Bridge in April when the river was low and the sun shining. I could see all the fish in the pool below and, as far as I could judge, every one had fungus, or the beginnings of it, on its head. By May, recovery had started as the water warmed, but only those whose infections had not progressed beyond the head were able to survive. We caught a number of fish after that with the obvious signs of healed-over lesions on their heads.

Imagine my surprise when looking through the Wark fishing book, kindly lent to me by Jennifer Lovett some time ago, at finding a letter from my father, addressed to Jennifer and referring to Colonel Mike Ryan, the Superintendent of the River Tweed Commissioners, also known as 'Bomber' Ryan because of his tendency to blow up blocking caulds with dynamite. His name is not to be mentioned in Selkirk, where his most infamous explosion took place:

> When UDN started in 1967 I tried to tell Mike Ryan that I had seen it before in 1938. He was adamant it was something quite new. I wish I had had your figures to show him then! I have vivid memories of 1937 as I caught 96 salmon to my own rod in the April school holidays. If my sister Rachel had not elected to get married on the last day of the holidays, I would have got to 100.

My father would have been seventeen in 1937 and, even writing all those years later, was clearly still irked by the absurd notion of his sister getting married, and in London of all places, when there were fish to be caught.

A look at Wark's book for 1938 reveals the extent of the disease. One comment at the end of March 1938, when the water would have been cold, just as in 1967, says, 'Fish all diseased.' Wark in February 1938 caught ninety salmon, but with the onset of disease in March, when the fish were dying and would not take, just thirty-one were caught. More evidence comes from the Revd William McCallum who, when not tending to his flock, wrote idiosyncratic summaries in the local press of the fishing year on the Tweed. For 1938 he wrote, 'In a river full of fish, drought and disease were against sport in the spring.' Then again, 'On the first of March, a most un-lionlike month this year, the Duchess of Roxburghe caught 3, including a fresh run 17-pounder, and fagged the fins [what does that mean!?] on other days, but disease raged.' Then later, 'Spots of disease were on every fish', and later still, 'In beautiful (warmer) weather, disease began to wane and the fish to recover, and on 14th April at Hendersyde Col. Taylor caught 12 to his own rod.'

It sounds just like the 1967 outbreak, and that my father was most probably right, and Colonel 'Bomber' Ryan wrong. We will never know for sure. The 1938 outbreak appears to have been short-lived, even if it would hardly have been given priority by the local press between 1939 and 1945. In a week or two, here in 2013, as things warm up, it would be nice to say the same thing: that it is over.

WINTER

It is a long old winter in this part of the world. Some say that the Danish *hygge* is the way to go, just accept that much of the day will be spent hugger-mugger in front of a log fire, or skulking by the Aga in the kitchen.

Winter's saving grace is the anticipation that mounts as we near the promised land that is spring, even if, when the inevitable north and east winds set in, any real warmth is a very long time coming. Fishers traditionally spend time tying flies for the next season, dreaming of the promise to come, either in a pool with salmon jumping everywhere, or with trout gobbling every mayfly that floats downstream. Some favourite old fishing tomes come out from the bookshelves, so that fishing vicariously from your armchair, glass of whisky in hand, slippers on and a log fire blazing, can be a wonderful comfort and second best to the real thing.

As for the salmon, in many ways it can be the most important season, with worries as to whether the spawning will be good, will the eggs hatch and the young alevins* and fry survive the inevitable winter floods? The evidence is that somehow enough make it, although in 2015–16, for instance, with a succession of massive floods one after the other, there was distinct evidence of reduced numbers when the fry sampling was done the following summer. As so many young salmon die before getting to sea anyway, it may be that there is some compensation mechanism that ensures higher survival rates apply in the river when numbers are reduced by such natural events, so that there may be no direct correlation with smolts going to sea, and returning adults a year or two later. Luckily, the wild-salmon world is built on oversupply (just one female can produce 15,000 eggs), so that there is great natural

---

* Newly spawned salmon still carrying the yolk.

capacity to recover, probably the only reason the Atlantic salmon still survives – albeit just – as a species.

My own winter is as yet incomplete, and only God knows how long I have left until my stumps are drawn at the end of the day's play and I join Freddie, after his long and lonely vigil, in the Cornhill graveyard. It has become a function of my winter that I become angrier, more grumpy at the folly of man and at the iniquities that the human race has inflicted, and goes on inflicting, on the natural world. I have no idea if it is too late for our Atlantic salmon ever to again reach the numbers that used to come back to our Scottish rivers in the 1950s and 1960s, but if the estimates of some are correct that there are now only 1.5 million left, on both sides of the Atlantic, then they might already be in danger of extinction. In the 1980s, just forty years ago, some estimates then had numbers closer to 10 million.

Before my winter closes, I pray for some comfort that both changes in human behaviour and the higher priority given to an iconic species by governments will give me reasonable assurance that the Atlantic salmon will not only survive but begin to recover sometime soon towards its former abundances. Success will depend on the efforts of my children, Richard and Nicholas, their wider age group and the generations after them. They will need great tenacity, single-mindedness and a good slice of luck to get the Tweed's fabled salmon runs back to anywhere near where they were when I was but a lad. I wish them all possible good fortune.

Uncle George

My father's younger brother George, the last of the seven siblings, died before I was born. By all accounts he was the most gifted of them all, as a wildlife photographer initially, but who knows what he would have become if, like so many young men, his life had not been cut short. Here is a little bit of his story, assembled in 2014.

After another frustrating fishing week, too much water and too few fish, I hope it is forgivable, on this Remembrance Sunday a hundred years after the First World War began, to look away from the river, and tell a sad story of the Second World War, no doubt one of millions such.

I returned this morning from laying a wreath at Coldstream's war memorial on which is inscribed, among too many others in this small Borders town, under those who fell 1939–45, the following: 'Home, The Hon George D. F/O'. Uncle George, my father's younger brother.

Another uncle, William, takes up the story from his autobiography:

The last child, George, arrived at The Hirsel two years later, introduced by Dr Fisher. In due course, he travelled down to England for his education, but he never went to Oxford as his brothers had, because, at the conclusion of his time at Eton, he went straight into the Air Force, only to be lost in 1943 when training off the coast of Canada. Because he was the youngest, and without much doubt the most attractive of the brood, his disappearance struck my parents very hard. Yet he was hardly ever mentioned in the family thereafter. This may sound strange, I concede, but is not so in my family. The fact we did not discuss his death did not mean we had forgotten him. Quite the reverse. Somehow, by some strange process, we succeeded, through our reticence, in keeping him alive.

I saw him last in Torquay, I dressed as a private soldier, he in Air Force uniform, before he went to do his training in Vancouver Island. From my billet down in Kingsbridge, I reported to my parents on his cheerfulness and general well-being, and suggested to them in Coastal Command, for which he was training, he might have a chance of coming through the war in one piece.

Three months later, word came through that he was missing. Evidently fog or some Pacific storm had swallowed up all the planes in his training flight, and they had not returned to base.

I do not think of him in that predicament, however. I remember him as I last saw him, smiling goodbye in a Torquay street, his forage cap set at a jaunty angle.

No doubt my father would remember him as he saw him on his final leave, walking down towards the lake with Mr Collingwood, the butler, talking sixteen to the dozen, disappearing into a hide with his camera, and then dispatching his companion back towards the house, coat tails flapping in the wind, still talking, so that the Great Crested Grebe would think that George was still with him, because birds cannot count.

I used this portrait of him in my play *The Dame of Sark* when Colonel von Schmettau, German Commander of Guernsey, told his prisoner of his last meeting with his youngest son, killed on the Russian front, and proudly showed the Dame a photograph of a Great Crested Grebe.

When I think of George's death, I think too of a line of Siegfried Sassoon's, brought to my attention in another context:

> Remember this one afternoon in Spring
> When your own child looks down and makes your
>   sad heart sing.

George and his flight, some eighty years later, have never been found. His name, this time 'Flying Officer The Hon. G. C. Douglas-Home', is marked on the Ottawa War Memorial in Canada. He went missing, presumed dead, on 14 June 1943, aged twenty.

They Never Had a Chance

For some reason, I have always been able to recall the Cuban Missile Crisis. I and my teammates were on a bus travelling from my prep school at Aysgarth in Yorkshire to play another school at rugby or football, I cannot remember which. The wireless was on in the bus. It was 1962 and I was twelve. I thought we were all going to die as President Kennedy called Krushchev's bluff. Ever since then, I have considered it most unlikely that I would lead my life without there being some cataclysmic conflagration. That I have done so, thus far, is incredibly fortunate. This is a little story, written first in 2014, of those who were nothing like so lucky.

Within the Royal Military Academy, Sandhurst, lies the Royal Memorial Chapel.

I spent a very happy, and reflective, two hours there yesterday, witnessing the marriage of a young Scots Guards officer to a general's daughter. The time before and after the actual ceremony gave me time to observe and consider.

Inscribed on the pillars within the chapel, under the heading of each regiment, were the names of those officers who had trained as cadets at Sandhurst, and had fallen in the Great War of 1914–18.

Next to our pew was the Durham Light Infantry, and on the pillar in front the Wiltshire Regiment, among the many others all around the chapel. The ranks and names of the officers who fell were listed in year order, those in 1914 first, going through the years until 1918, then some in 1919, who perished later from wounds suffered in the previous four years.

I was struck by the numbers, somewhere between twenty-five and forty officers in each regiment, by their ages, a preponderance of second lieutenants and lieutenants, most of whom would have been intolerably young and, by the same surname often appearing more than once, probably brothers.

Below the Great War list, on the west side of the pillar next to our pew, was an equally poignant addition of an officer killed recently in Afghanistan.

It was a beautiful day and, as the bride and groom paraded out of the chapel, through the guard of honour of six Scots Guardsmen in magnificent full ceremonial dress, pipes and all, through the milling crowd of guests, towards the War Memorial, the August sun beating down, it was a joy to reflect on such hope and happiness amid such a moving memorial to the horrors and tragedies of the past.

Then we walked from the chapel to the reception, with polo being played on our left and the passing-out parade ground on our right, to the marquee by the lake.

A habitual curmudgeon, and complainer about any social gathering requiring my attendance, it must have been the juxtaposition of the present joy of two brave and charming young people getting married, in those peerless surroundings within the background of that catalogue of the slaughter of so many young lives that made me realise how lucky we were and my grumpy-old-man-ness had to stop. It was a wonderful day and a privilege to have been included.

Tomorrow at 11 p.m., exactly a hundred years ago, after Belgium had been invaded, Britain declared war on Germany. As a consequence, all those young men's names are inscribed for evermore in Sandhurst's Memorial Chapel.

It has rained here, a hundred years later, the Tweed has risen a bit, there are signs of salmon coming into the beats just above the tide, and with more rain forecast this week, fishing may soon begin in earnest in 2014. When it does, and when you are into a 20-pounder and that little capsule, that bubble we all inhabit, is taking on a rosier hue, spare a thought for the events of a hundred years ago and the turmoil that engulfed the world and the millions of lives lost over the ensuing four years.

Many of those young Sandhurst officers would have been like us, keen fishermen. Unlike us, they never had the chance.

Robin

I have never been a great fan of poetry, at least partly because I am too stupid to understand much of it. My cousin Robin was an exotic and tragic character, hugely talented. He lived life to the full until he could take no more. I think of another cousin's wedding, the last time I saw him, sitting next to him in the church: I, an innocent and inexperienced boy, and he, a godlike figure. What follows is my sort of poetry; it makes me laugh. I wrote this first after a desultory salmon season in 2016, hoping, forlornly as it turned out, for better in 2017. It was intended to cheer up the piscatorially depressed.

Midst the pervading gloom of oncoming winter and uncertainties in almost every quarter of life – Syria, Brexit, Trump, Putin's sabre-rattling, the SNP ever threatening Indyref2, and, of course, our salmon (or lack of them) – it is time to depart, for the off-season, from matters Tweed.

We need some jolly, non-fishy preamble to the imminent festivities.

My cousin, Robin Douglas-Home, died on 15 October 1968, aged thirty-six, far too young; impossibly charming, enamoured of two princesses, one Swedish, one British, jazz pianist and friend of Frank Sinatra, journalist and author of the wonderfully titled novels *The Faint Aroma of Performing Seals* and *Hot for Certainties*. I am told that the Swedish royal family's objection to him marrying their Princess Margaretha was that he was a commoner. Well, quite!

He married the model Sandra Paul, now Mrs Michael Howard, and I hope their son Sholto will forgive me if I reproduce a rare poem, a little gem, written by his father and contributed only 'to his Firm's House Journal'.

I am indebted to a great friend, Jane Fellowes, also Robin's cousin, for finding and sending it on to me. It is a bit of fun, especially if you are of a certain age and can recall the ads that pervaded the ITV channels in the 1960s. Many of the names are still about today.

On the firm ground that we have all by now had enough of this year, it has nothing whatever to do with fishing.

Its title is 'The Copywriter's Romance' and here are some of the best bits:

> A Sanpic-scented summer's night
> A Persil moon above
> The Milky Way shone Omo bright
> He fell in Lux-washed love.
>
> Her rosebud lips were Revlon-Red,
> And blue-as-Daz her eyes
> A Eucryl-set of Gleeming teeth
> Proved she was Wisdom-wise.
>
> He judged the moment ripe and said:
> 'It's Ultra-clear that we
> Are deep in love (like Bread and Stork),
> So will you marry me!?'
>
> Haig-vaguely answered she, 'It all
> Depends what Daddie thinks –
> I've got no Pride or Gumption and
> My cooking Airwick stinks.'
>
> The Burton-groom looked Esso-smooth,
> Ryvita-slim the bride,

So Yaxa-cool in Surf-white tulle,
Walked Dolcis by his side;

And as they Daimler-drove away,
She said, 'A Player's please –
And now for Winalots-and-lots
Of little Hennessies.

Was he possessed of too much talent and charm? I met an old friend of his many years later on a day's shooting way up north in Scotland. He told me all about Robin, so many stories of their London days, as we bowled along in the back of a Land Rover between drives. It was fifteen years after Robin died. His old friend could not contain his tears.

Biter Bit

We all enjoy our sports, often ignorant of the very real dangers that accompany them. The obvious include being shot by a fellow 'gun' in the line, a greater risk when shooting grouse because they fly so low, or, while fishing, falling into the river and putting oneself at the mercy of some overpowering currents. Even to experienced practitioners, there are other more obtuse but almost equally shocking and dangerous possibilities.

It was bound to be, I suppose, after sixty years of it not happening. My father was the same, after over fifty years of shooting every game bird in sight.

He had always been good. His loader, the famous Six Mile Bottom gamekeeper Charles South recorded in *Old Gamekeepers* that he shot 100 wild cock pheasants with 100 shots at Stetchworth in one drive in the 1960s, 'and he never missed one, that was some shooting, I can tell you!' But if anything in his fifties and early sixties he was in his prime. He rented some shooting and a snipe bog, near where we lived, to entertain us. My lasting impression is that he never missed a snipe, by far the most difficult of birds to shoot with its jinking flight, let alone anything else. Annoyingly, he made it look absurdly easy. I used to ask him how he did it, to which he replied, 'Just shoot straight at them', which is like Tiger Woods saying to a golfer, 'Just hit the ball.' To give some idea of his dedication, despite three and a half years imprisoned by the Japanese, his game book records the green snipe he shot (borrowing a 16-bore) with a fellow officer, walking through rice fields in Malaya before he was captured when Singapore fell. He must have kept those records safely on him, and entered them in his game book when he returned home in 1945.

As all those who do it properly know, driven grouse are much more easily shot from the front, coming towards you, than after they have gone through the line. On this particular day, he shot one well out in front and immediately turned his attention to one of its companions, with his second barrel, in the rapidly oncoming covey. But before he could fire again, the first one, dead but falling fast out of the sky, got him squarely in the chest and laid him out in his grouse butt.

He was shaken and severely bruised, and could not move much for days afterwards, but he lived happily for many years and told the story against himself, with the accustomed twinkle in his eye. His friends were unsympathetic, universally of the view that it was high time one of those grouse got its own back.

Move forward a few years, the scene is the Learmouth stream, here at the Lees, late on a summer's evening, a joyous and quiet place to fish. Casting a long line as you must, I was wading up to my waist, down by the point from the north side, when a sudden unexpected gust of wind, mid-cast, threw my No. 10 Cascade treble, at some speed, into my right temple. I expected blood and lots of it, but there was none, just one of the three hooks well and truly embedded.

That was that for the evening's fishing, as I drove the forty minutes to the Borders General Hospital, arriving shortly after 10 p.m., and checked into A&E, while apologetically saying what a fool I was. The standard reply was 'There is no need to apologise. You should see what some of the idiots who come in here manage to do to themselves', which sent my mind racing down all sorts of inappropriate avenues. I strongly suspect I was one of those idiots, but it was kind of them to absolve me.

After some pulling and tugging, the kind doctor decided that cutting it out was the only option, the barb refusing to allow the hook out any other way. And so, halfway through his twelve-hour A&E shift, he took a knife to my temple and with some small incisions succeeded in getting the hook out, much to my, and I rather think his, relief. He offered me the fly but as the offending hook was battered, it found its way into the hospital bin.

After a stitch or two, and a tetanus jab, I bade the A&E team a grateful farewell and made my way home, eventually getting to sleep around 2 a.m., resting the left side of my head on the pillow to avoid the mildly throbbing pain on the right.

At the end of it all, I could not help thinking, even though I wear glasses anyway, 'What if it had gone into the corner of my eye?' We should all wear wraparound safety glasses, especially in a wind, but do we? Probably not.

Once in sixty years' fishing, at the age of seventy, I should be long gone before it happens again, as the good doctor, my saviour, kindly, if slightly unnecessarily, pointed out.

A Champion Ploughman

Just every now and then you meet someone who radiates goodness. I did not know Graeme especially well, but there was something so gentle, modest, calm and kind about him that you just recognised it. He adored his fishing. This is a tragic tale, but I am so pleased that he had a few moments of fishing heaven in his life. It was written shortly after his greatest triumph; the postscript is more recent.

This story is why we all go fishing. Despite its endless disappointments, just occasionally something remarkable happens, even in February. It was last week, Tuesday, 7 February 2017.

My wife Jane saw Graeme walking down to fish at 11 a.m. The next time he was seen was around 12.30 at the fishing hut, still visibly shaking having walked the ten minutes back from the Glide. Malcolm and Paul, the boatmen, had been rowing the other fishers in the Learmouth stream and Cauld stream respectively.

Graeme had had five casts in the Glide in that hour and a half. On the fifth, just where you would expect a pull, opposite the point on the other side, his line stopped, followed by ten minutes of nothing much, except something solid and unmoving attached to his fly. It was tied for him by Colin Pringle – Willie Gunn-like,* with a touch more shrimp in it, a medium-sized tube with a treble hook attached. The line was equivalent to a Wetcel 2 and his nylon 15-pound Ultragreen Maxima.

The water temperature was 38°F, the height on our gauge was 2 foot, perfect but with more water on its way for the afternoon.

---

* A Willie Gunn is a popular salmon fly.

Graeme is a Yorkshireman, ascetic in appearance, immaculately dressed, a quiet, unassuming, unfailingly polite and charming man. He is a fly fisherman through and through, and very good at it. Above all, a measure of the man, he would be embarrassed at me writing this.

After the ten-minute stalemate, Graeme's fish moved downstream, into the tail of the Glide where the water quickens as it falls away into the next pool, Cornhill Bend. Danger lurks there in the form of rapids and large submerged rocks, so he fought to stop it. Twice he thought it would go down, when both times it decided against. He saw its tail twice and knew he was attached to something unusually large.

He lost track of time as the fight continued, trying to be tough on it but not too much, and as he began to win, the gently sloping gravel became the problem. An easy place to land a normal fish, but with something so large, every time he brought it in, it touched the bottom, turned sideways and with the current acting on its flank, Graeme had no option but to let it go before trying all over again. Heart-stopping minutes followed, so near to success, but so far.

Eventually, he had the huge fish on its side, in the water, where he unhooked it, and his immediate thought was for its safety. It was a magnificent sea-liced cock salmon. Turning it upright, he held it face on to the current until he could feel it recovering, only then thinking of measuring it. Having laid it on its side, half covered in water, he placed his rod alongside, and scratched a mark on his rod opposite the nose. He righted it, and then allowed it to swim away, quietly and sedately, as big fish do.

Back at the hut, with Graeme still shaking, Malcolm measured the distance from rod butt to the scratch on the rod, reducing it by half an inch or so to be on the prudent side. It was 43 inches long,

109 centimetres. I have a cast of my 30-pounder in our hut, killed and weighed. Graeme said that mine was thicker than his. On the other hand his fish was longer and fresher, a sea-liced springer having much denser and heavier flesh than my autumn fish.

The Tweed chart puts a 43-inch fish at 30.2 pounds but has two crucial caveats. First, weight depends on the condition of the fish and, secondly, accuracy of the chart is much worse for fish over 40 inches. We are torn – are we not – between wanting certainty of weights for big fish, while not wanting to harm such a magnificent springer. Graeme's phone battery had been flat and he had left it in the hotel to charge, so there were no pictures for him to keep, which is sad. Pictures, however, do little or nothing to resolve the precise weight issue, except to confirm that the fish was big.

It is in our book at 30 pounds, the smart money being that it could have been anything between 28 and 32. Alas, for Graeme and for us, we shall never know.

It is a fishing story of epic proportions, a 30-pounder on 7 February. 'No pictures, on his own, not weighed, we have heard it all before,' I hear you say. But you have not met Graeme. If you saw for yourself, as we did, the undoubted emotion and veracity underlying his recounting of what happened last Tuesday morning, you would believe every single small detail of it. As I do.

Postscript

Just over three years later, Graeme died in an accident on his farm in Yorkshire. He had been here in February 2020, but the incessant gales and rain meant there would be no repeat of his previous successes. To occupy his time he would go off with his hiking boots and backpack on a twelve-mile yomp around Coldstream. He was the fittest of men. That was the last time I saw him. So modest that it was only after he died, in the most moving obituaries, that I learned that he was a World Champion ploughman, much loved and respected by all in his native Yorkshire.

Apart from his monster in February 2017, I remember he caught numbers of large summer fish in the week of my eldest son Richard's wedding in June 2016. His favourite places, where he caught most, were in the middle pools, which are all wade-able; he liked to be on his own. But for this hellish bug he would have been here in May, June and July 2020 with his best friend Terry Harper. Terry would be the first to say that it will never be the same without Graeme.

The Best of It?

It may be clichéd to portray the past as better than the present. In the salmon world, cliché or no, it most certainly was. I have spent much of my life trying to ensure, within very limited capabilities, that my beloved Tweed is in as good shape for the future, if not better, than when I was a lad. With serious ups and downs along the way, and if we can solve the ever present problem of our warming climate and its impact on our cool-water-loving fish, I hope it can be done. Sadly, the further south a river, the more unlikely that it will ever fully recover. What follows was written after another poor (and very hot) year in 2018, but shows both what has been possible in this great river, and how lucky my generation has been.

As one does at my age, I got talking to an old friend the other day about whether we have seen the best of it. That could apply to anything because those of us over pension age, pre-, during-, or post-war baby boomers, have been lucky. Inevitably, the conversation turned to salmon.

He recalled being sent to fish at Upper Floors on 1 February in the 1950s or 1960s, no matter which. It was freezing, so cold that nobody else wanted to go anywhere near the river. Every three or four casts he had to unfreeze the rings on his rod. He caught ten sparkling bright spring salmon and many more kelts. He killed all the salmon. It is what we did in those days; we never gave it another thought. They were days of plenty, we thought, and if we thought about it at all, we assumed that the 'plenty' would never end. Had you mentioned the words 'catch and release', nobody would have known what on earth you were on about.

The fishmonger's van would come round all the main Tweed beats before lunch and pick up the previous day's catch from the fish larder. Everything that could not be eaten was sold. As late as the 1970s, I remember the van arriving at Knockando on the Spey to collect the fishy bodies laid out in serried ranks.

That famously great salmon fisherman, Major John Ashley-Cooper and his friends took Rothes on the Spey throughout the 1950s and 1960s for the whole month of April. They paid the rent by selling the salmon they caught. There is a throwaway line in one of his books that I have never forgotten: 'When I caught my two thousandth Spey salmon . . .'! The Spey was just one of the many rivers he frequented. My father gave up keeping his fishing book when he had caught three thousand salmon. He and the major were in the salmon fishers' Premier League, if the major rather more like Liverpool or Manchester United compared with my father's Southampton or Stoke City.

Nostalgic conversations, such as mine with my friend, can become maudlin. Have we indeed seen the best of it? Will those days of plenty ever return for our children and grandchildren to enjoy, as we and our parents' generation did? Are our children and grandchildren going to miss out . . . again?

We were gloomy at the prospects for our salmon rivers. Just as our forefathers destroyed so many rivers with the Industrial Revolution, with impassable dams, with pollution and with over-fishing, now we are doing exactly the same with runaway global warming and the massive proliferation of fish farming in the sea. Whenever we humans have to choose between saving our wildlife – in this case our incomparable salmon – and profit, we opt for profit.

A map of where Atlantic and Pacific salmon are still thriving will show the remaining strongholds retreating ever more northwards. There were once salmon aplenty in northern Spain, in all west-coast French rivers and in those European rivers flowing northwards into the North Sea. The Rhine was coming down with salmon not so long ago. Ninety per cent of the rivers known to have healthy salmon populations are now in the four northernmost countries of Norway, Iceland, Scotland and Ireland. Yet so myopic are we that the Scottish government is even now, despite all the history of salmon destruction, guilty of presiding over almost every river on the west coast of Scotland being in the most endangered category. Why? Because of fish farming and its appalling effects on the wild-salmon population: sea lice proliferate and spread beyond the cages, killing wild fish, and massive numbers of fish also escape, leading to diseases being passed to natural salmon stocks and genetic mixing between the two. It is a matter of the utmost despair that we never learn the lessons of the past.

If there is another sin of which we are all guilty, it is 'shifting baselines', by which we manage to convince ourselves that things have not really declined as much as they have. What we should be doing is comparing the numbers of salmon with those of 50, 100 and 150 years ago. Instead we compare the numbers with last year's and five years ago and we ignore the evidence that fifty years ago the Faroese and the Greenlanders were catching not thousands of our salmon, but thousands of tonnes of our salmon, as were our own river and coastal nets, the North East and Irish drift net fisheries and numerous others. Poaching was rife, yet still there were plenty of salmon for the anglers to catch in the rivers. Now there is almost no netting anywhere and yet most of our rivers are not full of fish. I have seen estimates that Atlantic salmon numbers have dropped from 10 million to 1.5 million over the whole North Atlantic, and from 1.5 million returning to Scotland in 1971 to 250,000 in 2020.

The most easily digestible example of the decline over fifty to a hundred years is my old friend, metaphorically speaking, the Wye Wizard, Robert Pashley. He caught over ten thousand Wye salmon between 1906 and 1951. In 1936 he caught 678 salmon to his own rod, almost all on a fly. Twenty-nine of that ten thousand odd were over 40 pounds.

Now, the total annual Wye salmon catch is somewhere between 200 and 1,000, with little sign of improvement despite extensive remedial works being done over the last twenty years. The depressing reality is that Mr Pashley's great- and great-great-grandchildren have almost zero chance of seeing the Wye return to what it was in his day. We humans, nobody else, have caused that.

Until governments, such as the Scottish government and its abysmal fish-farming failures, take this appalling and continuing decline seriously and recognise it for what it is, my friend and I are not hopeful for the future of our salmon rivers. It is easy to blame politicians, but it is they who hold the power, and they who must show the leadership needed to slow and reverse the decline. But will they? History provides little comfort that they will, or that they even really care.

Why the Wye?

Of all the great British salmon rivers, the Wye was by any standards among the best. On 10 March 1973, when I was a guest of Tricia Davies and her father Edward, my fishing book records two salmon caught in the Cabalva Pool near Hay. They weighed 15 and 12 pounds, and another was lost; they were magnificent silver springers, exactly what the Wye was famous for. My hazy memory recalls a brief attempt at Erwood, then a day at Cadora further downriver, both of those in the 1970s. I have never been back.

History shows us that once the volume of fish in a river declines to a certain low point, it is the very devil to get it back. The smart thing is to stop the decline before it becomes terminal. It can be done. Sadly there are people in the salmon world who will continue in their self-centred way, fishing with no regard to the future, as if nothing has happened. The appalling drop in figures on the River Wye needs to be widely disseminated so that lessons can be learned. Be prepared for a shock.

Stephen Marsh-Smith was a regular fisherman here on the Tweed, and was kind enough to ask me to join his friends on such stellar fishing trips as Islamouth on the Tay. We caught twenty-four between us one September day. I got one in the Ash Tree, just above the bridge. It was 19 pounds and spent most of the fight trying to go downstream through the bridge arch on the other side of the river. That I stopped it was a triumph, deserving of applause, had it not been a solitary unspectated struggle. I took a bow nonetheless.

Stephen was a superb fisherman, considered and thoughtful in his approach, analytical, as befits a good dentist with a string of academic qualifications. He was completely charming but it seems he must have been a handful to be married to and had acquired a wife or two along the way. My mother liked him, but insisted on calling him 'Bluebeard', a little extreme even for my very proper mother. Stephen might have had a few wives but, as far as I know, they all lived happily ever after, unlike the former Mrs Bluebeards.

His passions were fishing and the Wye. He called his dog Pashley after the greatest Wye fisherman of all time. Stephen died in 2020, far too young at just sixty-nine, and was still working at saving the Wye until the end. To the far-off spectator, and from my intermittent meetings and conversations with him over the years, it seemed that if he could not save the Wye, get it back to something like its former glories, then maybe nobody and nothing could.

The gloomy thought is that when rivers decline to such a level, nothing will ever get them back. Good folk have been trying to establish a meaningful run of salmon into the Thames for as long as I can remember. Success, if any, is marginal. The same can be said of attempts to reintroduce salmon to the Rhine, the Loire, the Dordogne and so many other great European west-coast rivers ruined by man's 'economic progress', and which were strongholds of *Salmo salar*, to give the Atlantic salmon its formal name, over two hundred years ago.

Here are some figures for the Wye:

Robert Pashley's total Wye catch (1906–51):	over 10,000 salmon
Robert Pashley's best year's catch (1936):	678
Robert Pashley's number over 40 pounds:	29

Best annual rod catch:

1960s	1967	7,864
1970s	1972	7,433
1980s	1988	6,401

1990s	1994	2,100
2000s	2008	1,000
2010s	2016	1,665

Average annual rod catch:

1997–2020	Under 1,000 (lowest (2002): 357; best (2016): 1,665)

Estimated total rod catch:

2020	600

They make sobering and depressing reading. Looking at the long-term figures for catches, something seems to have gone wrong in 1990, from which numbers have never recovered, bar one glimmer of hope in 2016. Vast sums have been spent by the Wye and Usk Foundation and its partners in opening up blocked tributaries, in knocking down weirs, in providing new fish passes, in stopping pollution from slurry and in improving all-round water quality, in lime-ing acidified streams to bring them back into productivity, and a host of other things. Stephen was the moving force, the inspiration behind all these vital initiatives, over his twenty-plus years in charge.

No doubt everything done has had a beneficial effect, but the big question is whether the Wye will ever get back to anything like its former prolific self. Just at the moment, you might bet against it.

Playing the Cards

If my bridge-playing career has taught me anything, it is that you cannot choose the cards you are dealt. The dealer deals, you pick up your cards, arrange them as you see fit, and then make the most of them. That is the game; it is very simple. I spent a whole year at Oxford consistently having the worst hands; no paranoia here, it was true and acknowledged as such by my friends who quickly learned to groan when the draw had me as their partner for the evening. So it is with life: we are dealt hands and our job is to get on with it, especially in the seemingly random matter of our own health.

I know I should have gone sooner, but earlier tests had been inconclusive, with quite low prostate specific antigen counts. This one was just 5.6, so I nearly did not check it out either. Off to the Borders General Hospital, where a consultant with zero bedside manner, having extracted his hand from my bottom, announced, 'Seventy-five per cent certain you have cancer of the prostate.' That was it, very little sympathy, matter of fact, and a later biopsy proved he was right.

That was the start of nearly three years of various treatments, first an operation to remove the prostate, then radiotherapy to kill off any nasty cells still left, then testosterone suppressant injections once every three months for two years, because prostate cancer likes testosterone and struggles to survive without it.

I was diagnosed in 2018, had the operation and, just after I returned home, we had friends to stay for a wedding. I needed cheering up and one of our guests told this story. It struck a chord, as most silly jokes do in my life, and got me back to not feeling sorry for myself. It is an essential part of what follows, for even a modicum of success, the slightest titter of a laugh, that you do not skip to the end . . . or at least not until you get there in your own good time:

'Mummy, mummy are you *really* sure that I am a polar bear and not a brown bear?'

'Yes, my boy, I am quite sure that you are a polar bear and not a brown bear.'

'Mummy, mummy are you *really really* sure that I am a polar bear and not a black bear?'

'Yes, my boy, I am quite sure you are a polar bear and not a black bear.'

'Mummy, mummy are you *really really really* sure I am a polar bear and not a grizzly bear?'

'Yes, my boy, I am *really really really* sure you are a polar bear and not a brown bear, a black bear or a grizzly bear. Why do you ask?'

'Because I am fucking cold.'

I am writing this just after receiving my last injection. The effect, and the restoration of my testosterone levels, will take about nine months. Only after that will we know for sure if the cancer has gone for good, or whether something else will be needed if some of those nasty cells have somehow survived the battering they have been given. I am moderately fatalistic about it, and almost expect to have more treatment coming my way. 'Not to worry,' I am told. 'Even if it is still there, the aim is to keep it at bay so you will die of something else.' This is oddly comforting, sufficiently vague and aimed at persuading me that the present enemy may not be the one to worry about after all.

Throughout it all, the standard of care and expertise has been extraordinary. What luck to be around in an age when so many things can be dealt with. How many of us seventy-plus folk would still be here if we had lived a hundred, let alone two hundred, years ago? Very few. Something would have gathered us by now.

None of the treatments has been without its issues. The operation makes incontinence more likely; the radiotherapy makes that even worse, and also tends to mess about with your insides, which can become inflamed in the process of killing both healthy and unhealthy cells. The testosterone suppressant leaves you weak, any muscles disappear and the hot flushes are seemingly endless. Feeling low, irritable and depressed, absent any testosterone, can also be a major issue, so I have tried my best to counter any descent into gloom – not that easy in the depths of November and December darknesses.

But then the pluses are immense. First, I am still around and able to do most things, even if the distance I hit the golf ball is a hundred yards short of what it was. Secondly, I am so much luckier than many of my friends whose encounter with this terrible cancer blight has been far more severe. I feel guilty that I have been so lucky. However bad, the chances are there are always others much worse off than you, something emphasised by those I met, albeit briefly, in the hospital waiting rooms during the two months of my radiotherapy. Thirdly, and most strikingly, in the whole process of being ill, you meet extraordinary doctors and nurses whose whole purpose in their chosen careers is to make us better, to keep us alive and to do so with dedication, skill and good humour. Whatever we say is not enough, for how can you ever adequately acknowledge the saving of a human life?

Whatever gets me in the end, whether it is the residue of my prostate cancer or not, I know that I am in good hands, that whatever can be done to extend my life has been and will be done. We are all dealt a health hand, for good and bad. We must get on and play it to the best of our abilities.

What other choice do we have?

'Get over it, Dad'

Please forgive what follows. As I become older and more intolerant, my children (now aged thirty-eight and thirty-five) have to rein me in. They make me laugh with their cries of 'Get over it, Dad', 'It's a first-world problem' and 'Move on, Dad', as I rail against the iniquities carried out by others, often in my own garden. Here are just some that get my dander well and truly up.

We live in the most beautiful place. Our house stands in its own grounds on the outskirts of Coldstream. To the east, from beneath the 200-year-old beech trees, we look out over farmland. The river circles around us; on the opposite bank to the east, north and west lies England, with the Cheviot Hills beyond. To the west we have what we call 'The View', a depression cut through the ground and the surrounding trees, with a panorama from our front door straight onto the River Tweed as it flows, like a vast moving lake, all the way from Wark village.

Let's face it, by almost any standard, we are incredibly fortunate. That luck just goes up a notch or two if you happen to like fishing.

Michael Miller, whose family owns the Junction and Sprouston, rang a few years ago saying, 'This is very annoying.'

To which I replied, 'Hello, Michael, how nice to hear from you. What is annoying you?'

He responded, 'I have been reviewing the blurb we put on our website for the Junction, and we say we are the best, most productive beat on the Tweed. It isn't true, is it? You are! Your five-year average is now higher than ours.'

Ever modest, I pretended not to know.

'We shall have to change the wording,' he said, to which I replied that there was no need as I was sure that normal service would be resumed soon. But you get the picture; the Lees beat is good.

I mention all this so that any gripes and humour failures are seen in context. In short, I have drawn most of the aces in life's game of cards.

Some years ago, following the right to roam being introduced in Scotland, we agreed to a footpath going around our house and along the riverbank and being advertised in a local Coldstream Pathways booklet. There is signage, made by the council, and the idea is that everyone can walk through what is my extended garden as long as they all stick to the path. I maintain it, cut the grass and generally keep it all very tidy. Let me say first that there is a loyal and strong band of locals. I love to see them and they are most grateful for being able to walk here. I exempt all of them from the following.

First, there are the dog-pooh bags. So let's get this right: you take Fido for a walk; you take the trouble to put a pooh bag in your pocket; the adorable Fido does his business; you pick it up in said pooh bag; you tie it up carefully . . . And then you hang it on a branch of a tree, hide it in a tree's trunk or in a hedge, or you secrete it down a rabbit hole. What kind of lunatic logic is that?

You have introduced plastic, filled with Fido's pooh, into my pristine environment of a garden, and left it there for God knows who to clear up and take away. My language, every time I find another, can be interesting. I gather them up and bring them home to my bin. Oddly, in the forty years we have been here, I have never seen anyone in the act of doing it. We collect up to 150 of other people's dog-pooh bags every year.

Secondly, and this gets me going even more than the pooh bags, is when I am ignored. Because everyone who comes here is walking in my garden, I make a point of saying, 'Good morning', 'Hi, how are you?' or just waving hello if I happen to be on my tractor and the noise would drown out anything I say. There are those who not only give no response at all but look at me as if I have crawled out from under a stone. I can tell from the looks on their faces that they are thinking, 'Who are you to be talking to me?' I had son Nick with me once, during Covid lockdown. Even he, having seen an example of this at first hand, after initially advising me to 'Get over it, Dad', thought again. 'Why not tell them to get the f—k off my land?' and why don't we 'set the dogs on them'? It is just so staggeringly rude. Maybe they think I am a lowly gardener (I certainly look scruffy enough, and anyway gardeners are far from lowly), or even worse a council employee. We suppose that most of those who do not know think they are walking through publicly owned land in Comrade Nicola's own country. They are not, or at least not yet.

Thirdly, there are those who think that everything here is fair game. They pick my daffodils, my beautiful primroses and bluebells, take wood for their fires, sweet chestnuts and brambles to eat and conkers to play with in the autumn. One lady daily picked up my very large fir cones, which fall after a wind from a tree I planted. I watched her doing this for a few days before it got too much. 'Can I help you?' I said politely. She never came back. Driving in one day, I found a bicycle parked just off our drive, underneath the most magnificent sweet chestnut tree, 200 years old if it is a day. The cyclist was rootling about under the tree. I leaned out of my car window and uttered that time-honoured phrase, 'Can I help you?', to which he replied, 'They aren't very big, are they? I think I am a bit too soon. I will come back.' I replied that that might be fine if he came and asked me first, by knocking on our door. 'Oh,' he said. 'Do you think these are yours? Can you own them?' I replied that not only could I, but I did indeed own them; they were mine. 'You can't own a tree, can you?' he responded, to which he received a very sharp reply: 'Not only can you own a tree, but I do, and that sweet chestnut is mine.' He left looking somewhat puzzled, still trying to work out why I, as opposed to the people of Scotland, owned that tree. He, too, has not been back. All anyone has to do is ask and we would say, 'Of course, my dear fellow', or words to that effect. But nobody does.

Fourthly, litter. For some curious reason I am so used to it that it no longer offends so much. But it still irritates, provoking annoyance of the 'gloomily resigned acceptance' type. The summer is worst. I genuinely like to see the young out here, and enjoying the sunshine, in the most stunning surroundings. Yet bitter experience has taught me that after a sunny day I have to go on evening patrol to pick up the resulting litter, sweet wrappers, cans, plastic bottles, crisp packets, all the usual suspects. It is dispiriting. Who are their parents? Why do they think it is OK to leave their rubbish lying around, despoiling my lovely garden and grounds? If head boatman Malcolm Campbell spots it, he picks it up, drives into Coldstream, finds the culprits, hands over the litter with 'I think you left these behind' and a few other well-chosen words advising them never to do it again. I cannot turn on my TV without some self-righteous youth telling me how my generation has ruined the environment for them. These young eco-warriors do indeed have a point, but I would be more sympathetic if others of a similar age were not doing their level best to trash the place every time they walk through my garden.

On my son Richard's graduation from three years of boozing at Durham University, we were all seated in the Cathedral, bursting with pride at our various darlings receiving their degrees. Bill Bryson made the speech. He started with congratulations all round before moving on to his top-ten tips for success and good conduct in post-uni life. Numbers 1 to 5 were as you would expect: be generous and kind, considerate to those less well off than you, work hard, etc. He arrived at No. 6, with a pause. We knew something else was coming. 'If you find yourself walking down the street, and the person in front drops some litter and does not pick it up, you can, indeed must, kill them.' An odd instruction, you might agree, in the hallowed interiors of Durham Cathedral, but it was shocking, as he intended. That was all of fifteen years ago. Has anything improved on the litter front? Maybe, but my word, there is a long way to go.

Finally, there are those who deliberately ignore signage, especially with the word PRIVATE on it. We provide an excellent footpath, at no expense to the public purse, and yet there are those who will walk straight past the signs, down our drive and right in front of our house. One of the signs was thrown in the river. When asked did they see the signs, most either deny having seen them or become distinctly ratty at being advised they should not be there, standing almost on our front doorstep. Even in Scotland, the immediate curtilage of your house is private, by law, and the public has no right whatsoever to be there, especially when a perfectly good footpath is provided to circumvent the house.

So there you have it. I feel so much better having got all this off my chest. I can feel my children groaning at the silly old codger. But then I will bet both you, and them, that in twenty years' time, they will be just like me. Grumpy old men. And their children will be saying to them, 'Get over it, Dad. They are all first-world problems.'

And so they are.

Great Scott

Just upstream of my father's Upper Pavilion beat of the Tweed was Boleside. In the 1960s it belonged to the Scotts of Gala, Sir Walter Scott's kinsmen. Abbotsford lies on the south bank at the bottom of the Boleside beat. Curiously, Abbotsford and Sir Walter's descendants have never owned any salmon fishing, yet the Tweed defines the northern edge of Abbotsford's grounds, in full view of the house. The great man is said to have died in the bay of his dining room, lying with the window open, so that he could both see and hear the river from his bed. I cannot tell what else we might have had in common, but an abiding love of the Tweed, its salmon, its history, the noble art of fishing and the imperative of preserving it all for future generations would certainly have been one. I have tried hearing the ripples of the Tweed from the terrace outside the dining room where he lay on his deathbed, but I could hear nothing. As with so much in his life and writings, true or not hardly signifies; it is the story that matters.

I spent a very happy twenty years involved with Abbotsford, as almost the last man standing when Patricia Maxwell Scott died (1998) and her sister Dame Jean later in 2004. They devoted their lives to the memory of their extraordinary ancestor, Sir Walter Scott, the modern world's first great historical novelist. My wonderful colleagues as trustees of the bespoke Abbotsford Trust saved Abbotsford for the next century by collective hard work and skill. My motivation was mainly for Patricia and Jean, to whom I had made a solemn promise. My trustee colleagues did it for both personal and broader Scotland-wide reasons. They were magnificent, we had fun and made an unstoppable team. I have never been sure, strange to say, that today's Scottish people have ever really fully recognised one of their greatest sons. Will our work ever be appreciated by the mass of Sir Walter's own countrymen and women? Maybe one day.

Walter Scott was, bar his friend the Duke of Wellington, the celebrity of his time. Feted both here and abroad, everyone who could do so had read his books. With literacy rates so low, the number of books he sold was astonishing. Everyone wanted a piece of him, as the great and the good beat a path to the door of his Borders extravaganza, Abbotsford, on the banks of the Tweed in the heart of his beloved Borders countryside. It was the 'Delilah of his imagination', his 'conundrum castle', a spectacular folly and prototype for Balmoral and so many other Scottish baronial houses that now pepper the landscape.

His books and poems were the perfect travel brochures of their time. Even now, two hundred years on, the world has a vision of Scotland, of highland glens, bekilted warriors and fearsome clans, with the odd stag, aka *The Monarch of the Glen*, golden eagles and majestic lochs thrown in for good measure. He gave the ultimate Scottish romantic image to those living in more mundane surroundings in England and beyond. They poured north to see it all for themselves, and to some extent they still do.

It is extraordinary the number of Scots who if not ignorant of Scott are almost embarrassed by him. That they prefer and laud Burns is not in doubt, despite, even because of, his womanising and debauchery. Somehow it is in the Scottish psyche to empathise with the rascal, the underdog, the one who behaves badly and has few redeeming features – in the case of Burns, the genius of his poetry. In contrast, Scott was a faithful and devoted family man, a genuinely good bloke, but, alas, a Tory and a unionist.

Worse than that, he was a man of his word and of unbending probity. Sheriff in Selkirk for many years, he had a compassionate heart. His most trusted friend and employee Purdie came to work at Abbotsford after being up before him in court for poaching. When financial disaster struck in 1826, he owed the equivalent of £10 million in today's money. One suspects Burns would have walked away and left the creditors to pick up the bill. Scott said he would pay off his debts, 'my own right hand shall do it', and so he did, effectively killing himself with hard work in the process. He died at Abbotsford, looking out over his adored Tweed, in 1832, aged just sixty-one, worn out by the struggle. It is both a heroic and a tragic tale, yet, strangely, nobody has made a film of his life. Done well, it would be both joyful and a tear-jerker.

His books, unlike Jane Austen's, are seldom read now, despite many abbreviated and digestible examples being available. Because of my involvement and absolute need to know the subject, I studied the more famous ones, favourites being *The Heart of Midlothian* and *Rob Roy*, with *Waverley* and *The Antiquary* a little behind. I enjoyed them and, despite some slow beginnings, they are very readable.

Abbotsford itself is open to the public most of the year. There is a new visitor centre (of course) where Scott's story is beautifully told. Over 40,000 visitors come annually, continuing the pilgrimages that have been made since he died.

But still there is something in the Scottish character that prefers to look away, to pretend he never happened. So many will never love him because of his political views and because he enjoyed the company of so many English friends. All of which ignores that he was the most passionate of patriotic Scots, and has done more for the Scottish tourism industry, on which so many depend, than anyone else, even now, decades later.

But in our northern world you cannot be a Scottish patriot and a Tory and/or unionist; you cannot be a man of unblemished honour and probity, and you certainly cannot have loads of English friends. All of which says much of the political position in Scotland today, above all its small-mindedness. Which is ironic for the man whose words –

> Breathes there the man, with soul so dead,
> Who never to himself hath said,
> This is my own, my native land!

– are the epitome of patriotism. As for the idolised Burns, he could never have written,

> Oh, what a tangled web we weave,
> When first we practise to deceive!

Exactly how many children, both legitimate and illegitimate, did he have? Really? That many?

Great Scott!

A Tweedy Revolution

Stereotypes are often unfair. Nonetheless, anyone surveying the Tweed's fishy scene now would find it hard not to conclude that the rod-carrying, tweedy and Range-Rover-or-equivalent-driving fraternity have completely taken over, and have in the process confined to the history books those who worked on the nets for a living and caught, for food and for sale, as many salmon and sea trout as they possibly could.

The original Tweed Acts, promulgated by Lord Somerville of Pavilion and Sir Walter Scott in his Abbotsford lair, were passed in 1807. Unforeseen by their proposers, two hundred years later those Acts would hammer the first nail in the coffin of the livelihoods of those financially dependent on the river's bounty. Those higher up the river, who were more interested in both angling as sport and there being enough fish left to spawn and to be caught, had started an unstoppable revolution.

It was the first tentative step towards salmon conservation as we know it. These days, the killing of a wild salmon is rare. The historic extract below, from over two centuries ago, provides the greatest possible contrast. The sheer scale of the netting industry from Berwick right up to Kelso was staggering. To this day, in law, the primary right is to fish by net, not by rod and line, and upriver salmon-fishing proprietors could still legally net. They wouldn't dare though, would they?

What netting there is now on Tweed, just one part-time net at Gardo in Berwick's harbour, maybe catches 500–1,000 salmon and few more sea trout in a whole year. Even in the 1960s, 1970s and 1980s it was very different, with over thirty nets, some full-time, catching up to 100,000 salmon a year. From 1987 to the mid-2010s, these nets were bought out and closed down in the name of conservation. I was involved in all these buyouts myself and we thought at the time that thirty nets was bad enough, for in a dry summer little or nothing would get through to Coldstream and above. The nets would catch most if not all of them, until the August floods came along.

I am indebted to Ralph Holmes, the last of the major netting operators, for the following passage. His family, together with the Berwick Salmon Company, made netting on the Tweed their business, and a very profitable one, for many decades before 1987.

This extract dates from over two hundred years ago. If we thought there was a problem with fish getting through in 1987, we did not know the half of it. It comes from *The History of Berwick* by a good vicar, the Revd Thomas Johnstone, written in 1817, and entitled 'Exports-Salmon':

> The chief spring of the trade of Berwick is unquestionably the Salmon Fishery, which commences on the 10th day of January, and continues until the 10th day of October. Dr Fuller, in his History, says that in 1799 the rental of the Fishing Waters in the Tweed, from the mouth of the river to Norham, a distance of 7 miles, was about £10,000 yearly, at present the same distance is rented from £25,000 to £30,000. On this extent of river, 70 boats are employed, in each of which are 6 men, and from 400 to 500 fish are sometimes drawn ashore at one draught. The Fisheries lie on both sides of the river, although those on the south side are reckoned to be the best, and the limits of each water are distinctly marked out. The mode of fishing is thus described by Mr Pennant:
>
>> One man goes off in a small flat-bottomed boat, square at one end, and taking as large a circle as his net admits,

brings it on shore at the extremity of his boundary, where others assist in landing it. To it may also be added, that in the middle of the river is a large stone (or ladder) on which a man is placed, to observe what is called the Reck of the salmon coming up.

Previous to the year 1787, all the salmon sent to London from Berwick were boiled and put into Kits; but since then they have been sent in Boxes stratified with Ice, by which mode they are preserved for a considerable time. In the course of last year 10,215 Boxes of fresh salmon were shipped at Berwick, each box containing 6 stone, at an average of 11 shillings per stone. During the same period not less than 300,000 salmon, gilses [grilse] and trouts [sea trout] were taken in the River Tweed, the greater proportion of which was exported to London in Ice, the yearly expense of which amounts to £900.

Such figures are astonishing, and one can only imagine by how much they were underestimated when one takes activity on the river as a whole into consideration, with traps, leistering* and every other sort of legal and illegal activity, right up to Galashiels and beyond in the years before 1807 and the setting up of the Tweed Commissioners. No wonder the Upper Proprietors insisted that something be done to allow more fish through. The process of regulation and control of exploitation took another huge leap forward with the Tweed Act of 1857, many of the basic principles still applying today.

When all is said and done, and regardless of the rights and wrongs of how this has all come to pass, the fact is that commercial

---

* Spearing with a large trident by torchlight at night.

netting of salmon is all but extinct. A way of life, and means of making a living, has gone forever for many traditional netting families in the lowest fifteen miles of the river, and in Berwick especially.

Now the rod-fishing proprietors provide 99 per cent of the funding to the River Tweed Commission to run the river and generate a similar proportion of the income. Stranger yet, this is not from killing salmon but from catching them with rod and line, and putting over 90 per cent of them back in the river.

If you had predicted this state of affairs to the good Revd Thomas Johnstone, to Dr Fuller or to Mr Pennant, our informants of how it was over two hundred years ago, they would have thought you were mad. But that is exactly what has happened, and that is how it will remain for as long as our salmon keep coming back to this wonderful river. Wild salmon have become scarce, infinitely scarcer than they were when 420 men were employed for nine months of the year to net them.

None of this is the traditional netters' fault. It is rather man's contempt for the natural environment over previous centuries, but more particularly over the last fifty to a hundred years, that has made survival so much more precarious for our salmon. Until we can get a grip on global warming and reverse its impact, it is unlikely that what those scribes of yore wrote about, hundreds of thousands of salmon coming home to the Tweed, will recur.

Nature's compromised bounty is insufficient to allow unlimited harvest. It is the fault of humans interfering in and destroying the way nature would do things if left to itself. It is not those far-off netsmen that are to blame. They were, after all, just working hard to make a living. But they, and their traditional way of life, have paid the price; they are the collateral damage.

A Question of Numbers

I have an uneasy feeling that only those who care nought for catch numbers are truly rounded anglers. In which case, come the purist revolution, I would be exposed for what I am, a shallow and materialistic sham. What follows proves that, with no shadow of a doubt.

One of my very best friends, a man with a fine angling pedigree (inevitably attached to a wife with an even better one) was wont to announce at the start of any day's fishing, 'It's a question of numbers.' In other words, there was no doubt we were to catch some. It was merely a matter of how many. Even though we all knew he was jesting, somehow it started the day on the right note, outrageous optimism being a *sine qua non* of the home-based (as opposed to Russian) salmon angler.

Astoundingly, I have been fishing for salmon, exclusively in the UK and Ireland, for sixty years. I have been asked many times to venture abroad, but as we live within spitting distance of one of the best beats of the best salmon river in the UK, it always seemed a bit silly to use up some precious holiday, away from the office, paddling around in yet another river. I nearly went to the Alta in Norway, the only foreign river for which I would make an exception, as a guest of my old friend the Duke of Roxburghe, but had to call off when a nether-regions surgical procedure rendered me incapable of doing anything, other than lying down, for two weeks.

A large part of the reason is reluctance to pay. I try my very best to annoy friends by saying, 'I've never paid for fishing in my life and have no intention of starting now.' Not true, of course, because we used to keep two weeks in October and early November for my father and his friends right through the 1980s and 1990s, the opportunity cost of the rent we missed out on bringing tears to my oh-so-Scottish eyes.

I am asked, 'How many salmon have you caught?', especially when guests see my Smythson of Bond Street book lying around, for some reason usually in our dining room. Such a yesterday question. I have never told anyone, although my two boys may have a faint inkling – not that they are bothered. There have been good years, usually punctuation marks in my far-from-stellar career as an accountant: seventy in my gap year (1969), one hundred the year after I 'retired' (2007), or at least wound down from full-time occupation of an office, and quite a lot in lockdown year (2020), but it's too recent. Not telling you how many.

Reticence has much to do with upbringing. Someone once told me that numbers were vulgar, and even now, having exposed the modicum of info above, I feel a hot flush coming on. Will I regret it? Is anyone interested? For those who do not know, I spent thirty-five good years in my accountant's office, thereby seriously limiting angling opportunities, unlike those scions of old who seemed not to do anything but fish, 'office', like 'dinosaur', being a term, to them, from another world. We might never see their like, and the numbers of salmon they caught, again.

Just after the Covid 'lockdown', because the ghastly, unspeakable English were not supposed to be able to come over the Border (they did, but never mind), we found ourselves letting at short notice to those Scots who, many of them, had been, perforce, denied their annual Russian trip. Not only were they all completely charming (yours truly was briefly their ghillie) but my word, could they fish! Their tales of Russian derring-do, in something called 'the Yokanga' or another something sounding like 'the Ponoi', left my mouth hanging wide open, 100 salmon in a week, sometimes closer to 200, being not unusual. I would find myself suddenly going from not telling my catch numbers for fear of bragging, to not wanting to say because the numbers over sixty years were, in comparison, so pathetically puny.

The Duke, he who so kindly asked me to the Alta, used to tell me about the 30, 40 and 50-pounders he had caught. My slightly irked and feeble response would be: 'That's cheating. Anyone can catch those there. To really qualify you have to catch a 30-plus-pounder here.' Which, of course, non-swanks, I have. I did not know my post-lockdown new fishing friends well, but I would have said something like: 'That's cheating. Getting thirty a day in Russia, on the Yokanga or the Ponoi, anyone can do that. To qualify you have to catch ten or more in a day in this country, and on a fly only.'

I have done that six times, and numerous other days of eight or nine. Now I have gone too far. Far too much information and nobody likes a show-off. Delete before going to print? Maybe not. But at least there is one number I will never give up.

So there.

A Migration Miracle

This was written a few years ago after one of the most glorious and spectacular spring evenings you could ever enjoy on the banks of one of our great salmon rivers. If you did not know what you were looking for, or at, you might well have missed it, even though the procession was endless. The Tweed has no hatcheries and has not had for decades. This was a miracle of nature's very own making. The human role in it is simply one of facilitation, of keeping out of the way, of allowing the fish to get to where they want to go, and do it for themselves. It happens every year at much the same time, but this was by far the most spectacular example. If you are ever lucky enough, you may one day see for yourself what I mean.

Last Monday was glorious and, despite being a bank holiday, I spent much of it inside at meetings. Late in the evening, around 9.15 p.m., when the heat was gone and all was cool and quiet and there were no walkers, I wandered out to sit beside the river, just above our cauld. There is a bench, a most comfortable one, dedicated to 'Distillery Dave and his long-suffering wife' from his erstwhile fishing mates, the clue to his early demise being all too plain from the commemorative plaque.

All was calm, the light just going, a full moon in the south-eastern sky, the Temple Pool like a millpond, and a heron in its usual place on the edge of the cauld, picking off the odd smolt if one came too close to the side. Smolts had been running steadily for weeks, and very visibly in the low and clear conditions that had prevailed since mid-April.

Only when I had fully settled on Distillery Dave's bench did I notice the procession. Never had I seen anything like it. Thousands on thousands of smolts, myriad giveaway dimples in the smooth surface, each party about 10 to 15 feet in diameter, one after the other, posse after posse, some veering towards the dry edges of the cauld before sensing the flow towards the 30-foot gap in the middle. Through they went, no hesitation at all, down into the churning waters of the Cauld stream, and away.

It was mesmerising. Of course I have seen smolts migrating before, but nothing on this scale. Not just the numbers but the speed was astonishing. They were on a mission. I spotted each party about one to two hundred yards upstream, and they travelled that distance in no more than two minutes. I had heard evidence that caulds can hold up smolt migrations; not so here, they never hesitated, straight through that 30-foot gap without a pause. At that rate, they would be at Berwick and into the sea sometime the next day.

Head boatman Malcolm saw it, texting the following evening '1000s of smolts', so that massive migration continued unabated right through the next day. I wish you had seen it too; from Distillery Dave's bench, it was something. But maybe you are sitting in your armchair, theorising, glass in hand, about how useless river managers are and how you, personally, could put every river right, at a stroke, by building hatcheries, or salmon ranching or some such quasi-factory process.

Far from being the solution, the message from both sides of the Atlantic is that when we humans destroy a river's salmon run by pollution, building dams, overfishing, or whatever else we are so good at doing and ignoring the destruction we cause, the one thing humans do next is to try to correct it by massive hatchery projects. It does not work. The oft-quoted hatchery on the Tyne produces under 3 per cent of what comes back to the Tyne now; you can argue that initially a hatchery is needed to pump-prime where there are no fish at all, but even that is not certain, as some salmon naturally stray into rivers in which they were not born.

Perhaps the bigger question is how many of the thousands of smolts that I saw travelling seaward that evening would make it back in one, two or three years' time? It used to be up to 30 per cent and is now as low as 3 per cent. Theories abound as to why; none are convincing and even if we find out, how can we influence what happens in the ocean between here and Greenland?

It could come right again for reasons we shall never understand. I would want to be fishing if 30 per cent of what I saw that evening came back. You never know. There is a long-term natural cycle, so long as we humans don't continue messing it up by warming the planet: the new unknown, or as someone once said, 'a known unknown'. Climate change . . . again.

But at least there was hope: those myriad little migrants were carrying it in their tiny, less-than-six-inches-long bodies on their epic journey. Hope may be all we have, but in uncertain times for the Atlantic salmon's very survival as a species, thousands of little reasons for hope is a good start.

The Too Difficult Tray?

As I reach the end of this foray into a fortunate life, with one terrible exception, I am all too aware that I have written little or nothing about my immediate family. My father, yes, because he taught me fishing, shooting and cricket, at least two of those being great sustaining passions. Of my mother, my wife Jane and my two boys Richard and Nicholas, there are only passing mentions. Which is odd because between them they have been by far the biggest influences on my stumbles through life. This will not do any of them justice, but it is a fitting conclusion to this book. The best, the most important, should always be left until last. If this embarrasses them – though it cannot embarrass my mother sadly for she is long gone – then that is nothing new. I have been embarrassing my sons ever since Nicholas saw my battered old rusting Golf motor car turning up at his prep school bringing me to watch him play cricket, and walked smartly in the opposite direction. In his shoes I would have done exactly the same and, even if I cannot remember it, probably did. Difficult to write about my immediate and closest family? Perhaps. But too difficult?

My mother was Nancy Straker-Smith, born of a curious alliance between Thomas Smith and Edith Straker. They lived at Howden Dene just outside Corbridge in Northumberland where Nancy was born, as was her elder brother Billy. Thomas was a keen angler and they owned a beat of the Tyne. In the 1930s, because of pollution, caused largely by the burgeoning shipbuilding industry, the Tyne became devoid of all migratory fish. Ironically, Thomas was director of Smith's Dock Co., which was part of the source of the pollution. They upped sticks and moved to Carham on the Tweed, where there still were salmon, and plenty of them. I was told sometime

241

later that Sir Thomas, otherwise the most correct of men, had had a mistress in Newcastle for many years. I expressed shock, to which my interlocutor remarked 'Having seen your grandmother, are you surprised?' Well quite.

My mother escaped to the WRNS during the war, which she loved. Shortly after her return from war duty, she married my father in 1946 at Norham Church. They briefly moved to Duns, then to a farm at Easter Langlee outside Galashiels for over thirty years, thence to a bigger farm at Westnewton in North Northumberland, where they lived out their lives in great contentment.

Nancy had been a keen horsewoman and angler, catching two 30-pounders at Carham, but gave everything up to look after her husband and three boys. Never a very warm person (my previous interlocutor might have repeated, 'Having seen your grandmother, are you surprised?'), she was incredibly correct, bordering on the unbending, very 'proper' and a wonderful guide and mentor in bringing up three reasonably decent boys. If teased, she had a great sense of humour, but was at her happiest in a most orderly and structured life. Although devoted to each other, our parents gave little outward sign of affection, something passed on to us boys, so that hugging, even kissing, our mother was rare. This is not something of which I am proud. It was as if by not hugging and kissing her we were exacting some form of punishment for her own upbringing and her consequent lack of warmth. Although she had the life she wanted, I detected later, but too late, that she wished she had done more, spread her wings around the world. But she subjugated all to her husband, who never wanted to move very far from home after his wartime horrors.

In terms of character formation, if I were to say that I owed more to my mother than to any other single human being, she would have been surprised. She never put herself first. Despite my shameful retaliation in the 'warmth' stakes, I hope she knew that.

How do you write about your children? Standing at 6 foot 7 inches and 6 foot 6 inches respectively, they tower over their diminutive father at 6 foot 2. Now they are aged thirty-eight and thirty-five, the word 'children' hardly seems appropriate. I am immensely proud of them both in every possible way. An early lesson in the fragility of life and our own mortality, the death of Freddie cannot have left them unscarred. We would have spared them that for anything, but they have coped extraordinarily well or at least, like all of us, they have learned to carry on but never forget. I cannot help wondering what Freddie would have been, over thirty by now and over 6 foot 6 like his brothers? Who knows? They would have loved him.

Richard is a solicitor, married to Jaime ('Gem'), also a solicitor. They have two little (for now!) boys, Benj and Henry, and they live in Edinburgh. Nicholas, a media man, has also moved to Edinburgh, in a long line of D-Homes migrating north. Unmarried as yet, he is a much better games player than he ever knew. He has developed into a proper golfer, his iron shots, like a pro's, descending from some journey into outer space to make a crater on the greens. Richard, too, has one of the best golf swings you will ever see; maybe he will go back to it when his boys get the bug. Neither is especially keen on fishing – my fault for it being such a big thing for me – but I hope they will take it up more in later life. Luckily they are both bright and had no trouble with exams when they put their minds to it. Jane has been a much better and more affectionate mother to them than I could ever be a father. I find it difficult hugging my own children when they tower over me! I never thought I would suffer from small man syndrome.

Despite all that and the aloofness inherited from my mother and grandmother (her again – where is that shrink?), I love them both more than words can ever say, not that they will be able to read that last bit without feeling nauseous.

And now Jane. The very best of all should be last. We started badly, at the Northern Meeting at some hotel in Inverness. For Sassenachs, the NM is a Scottish reeling bonanza held twice a year in the environs of Inverness, the clientele being mainly temporarily migrating kilt-wearing toffs performing such ancient jigs as Hamilton House, the Reel of the 51st, the Foursome and Eightsome (some waggish heroes even enjoying a Sixteensome) reels, among myriad other such incomprehensible prances. As dyed-in-the-wool lowlanders, we don't think much of these things. I had come to stay with my old highland (well, Eton and Oxford) mate Philip Mackenzie at Farr, ill prepared for such jollity and high jinks. After much discussion, the Mackenzie clan decided, through gritted teeth, that there was nothing for it but to lend me a Mackenzie tartan kilt. Need one say, I spent most of the rest of the evening explaining to every clannish Mackenzie which peculiarly niche branch of the Mackenzies we Douglas-Homes came from.

At some point in the evening, my dance card blank, having failed the acid test of all reeling heroes in obtaining a pre-booked partner for each and every reel, I found myself propping up the bar with mine host, the younger of Farr. We were sorting the world out, as is one's wont on such occasions. Suddenly I spotted a face I knew, rare enough that far north, even more surprising it was a 'she', and a very attractive one too. After extracting myself with the greatest difficulty from my pole position at the bar, I approached Tina and introduced myself not only to her but also to her companion, one, or so I was to be told, Jane Pease. I subsequently discovered that my bespectacled, frizzy-haired (lots of it) self left said Jane Pease peculiarly underwhelmed. What of me? I can remember the whole thing, but only through a haze, the precise cause of which I can only leave the reader to guess. Of course I remember her, but it would be fair to say that on neither side was there the first suspicion of spark, as I retreated to further disconsolate deliberations at the bar, where the younger of Farr still lurked.

The scene moves on to some years later. I had moved to continue my stellar accounting career in Edinburgh rather than in London. Unknown to me, Jane had done the same, if not in the accounting world. Her flatmate Angela knew my cousin Walter Scott, and she kindly asked me to her drinks party. There Jane and I met again. Maybe it was the passage of time, maybe my hair was less frizzy and maybe I had not just staggered from a bar; whatever it was, she (generously) was not physically sick when she saw me again. I won't tell you what I thought, because you can work it out. A few months later, after a decent courtship, we became engaged. She says I uttered the ultimately romantic words, 'I suppose we had better get married then' (no, not for that reason!). That she agreed, as she has reminded me ever since, was because she was desperate, and not for any of my many admirable qualities. And so in 1980, on a peerless May day in the foothills of the Cheviots, we were married, as we remain over forty years later.

Let me tell you something of her background, for only then will you get the full measure of the person. Her father was Maurice Oliver Pease, 'MOP' to his friends, from a highly successful Quaker family, scions of the Stockton to Darlington railway. County Durham was and still is their patch. MOP married Jane's beautiful Polish mother Marysia when he was fifty-three. Up until then he had, by all accounts, 'put it about a bit' without ever being married. Marysia already had two children by a previous marriage, but her husband had died after the war, of injuries inflicted during the conflict. Jane was the only progeny of MOP and Marysia's marriage. Tragically, Marysia had developed cancer around the time Jane was born and died when her daughter was just five years old. Jane and her two 'halfs' were brought up by MOP and two consecutive stepmothers. With a father old enough to be her grandfather, and with no mother, it must have been very hard. Half-brother Andrew was her greatest ally, and remains so. He had lost both parents while still under ten.

Somehow, Jane emerged from all this, via school at St Mary's Wantage, from which she was expelled for selling gin, and stints in Edinburgh, for A levels, and London, as an extraordinarily well-adjusted and resilient person, the one I met again at Angela's party when she was twenty-three. She has always underrated herself, both in her physical appearance – she is beautiful, like her mother – and her considerable abilities and personality. My mother was not sure: like father like daughter, perhaps. She knew MOP by repute and did not like what she knew; she could be unforgivingly strait-laced. Somehow she could not believe that Jane would not have inherited some of what my mother viewed as her father's more disreputable characteristics. I never met either Marysia or MOP, for I married an orphan. MOP had died when Jane was eighteen.

Jane is a remarkable woman. Like any couple, we have had our moments, not least when Freddie died. However, at no point did either of us give any ground on total loyalty and underlying love and respect for the other. She is amazing. As a tribute to all her unique qualities, the final piece of this ramble through my life is written by her. It says it all, if it is rather less than flattering of me, which is only fair. There is not a word that I disagree with. Beautifully written, it says more of Jane than I could ever write.

So that's it, my family, the most important people in my life. Should I have allowed them to sneak out of the 'too difficult tray'? Only you, the reader, can objectively answer that. Ah well, it's done, too late now.

Freddie

Jane wrote what follows for *The Times*, six years after Freddie died at 12 noon on Saturday, 27 January 1990. It speaks volumes in every way. Even now, at the distance of thirty-two years, it is overwhelmingly sad. A surprising number of our friends have lost a child. They would agree that you never recover from the devastating loss, but somehow adjust to going on living, if with permanent regret, melancholy and enduring affection.

Freddie was born on 13 December 1989. He weighed 8 lb 13 oz on arrival and appeared to be both beautiful and healthy. Having had two boys, Richard and Nicholas, I had thought a girl would be nice, but once Freddie arrived it could not have mattered less. I had been sick all through the pregnancy and it was just wonderful to have the baby. Freddie had been my decision. Andrew did not want more children at that time, so the pregnancy was not as happy as it might have been for either of us.

The boys thought he was terrific. Andrew, who was very good with them as children, had never been great with small babies. Freddie was very much my baby, and I slept in his room. He was not a peaceful baby, and never slept for more than about three hours. On 27 January, he woke early. I remember thinking I must soon put him on his back so that he could look at toys, and perhaps not want food and company quite so early. We had to go to a wedding that day, and K, who helped with the children, was coming to look after them. Freddie did not settle so K took him for a walk. When she got back she said he had cried for ages, but was now asleep. I did think I might have picked him up sooner. We lifted the pram into the house, and K took off his hat and gloves. She muttered that she was relieved when he made a noise because he looked as if he was hardly breathing. I went off for a couple of minutes and then came to say goodbye before going to the wedding.

Freddie's little hands were totally white and I thought it odd that he was cold. He was lying with his face down on the cot mattress, which was unusual, and as soon as I picked him up I knew there was something wrong – but I could not believe he was dead. I screamed to K and tried hopelessly to revive him. The hospital is only half a mile away and Andrew drove us there as fast as possible. K had rung the doctors to warn them and they were waiting for us. They tried incredibly hard to resuscitate Freddie. They stopped only when I asked them to, because he would have been brain damaged, having been starved of oxygen for so long. The doctor and nurse were shocked and upset. It was a nightmare. I think I kept asking if he was dead. Eventually the doctor handed him back to me and said to take him home. I couldn't imagine what we were going to do with him, but they said it was so that we could all say goodbye.

I took Freddie to his room and held on to him. I didn't want to put him down. I remember thinking he couldn't be dead and would wake up. I thought I ought to change his nappy. Although I kissed and cuddled him, I did not look at his eyes. It was like holding an empty shell. Freddie the person had gone. Andrew came to hold him, and both boys kissed him goodbye. Veronica, a great friend and Freddie's godmother, came to support us and she held him. That was very touching – I'm not sure I could have done the same.

Two uniformed police arrived soon after we got home. They were tactful and waited in the kitchen. As it was a 'sudden death' the CID had to come from Hawick. They seemed to take hours to get here. I can't remember if they asked me anything. I certainly never got the impression I was under suspicion, but was relieved I had not been on my own and there were witnesses to testify I had not killed him. The police looked in his bedroom and at him. At some stage one of them told me I must put him in his cot and not carry him around.

Finally the undertakers came. They had only an adult coffin and when I put Freddie in, he looked so lost. I had wrapped him in a shawl, but by this time he was already cold and stiff. We watched the hearse take him away followed by a police car to escort him to Edinburgh for a post-mortem. Watching him go away was unbelievably painful, yet there was nothing I could do.

I do not remember much about the rest of the day. That night I moved back into our bedroom for the first time since Freddie was born.

Organising the funeral and all the technicalities was ghastly, but it did give us something to do. We wanted Freddie to be buried at Cornhill because the boys had been going to Sunday school there and we knew the vicar. However, Freddie had died in Scotland so that meant extra forms to fill in and journeys to Berwick. A great friend helped me choose the flowers for the coffin and made sure they were where I wanted them. The funeral was supposedly private, but good friends turned up and also people from the village I hardly knew and I was very touched. My brother drove all the way from Norfolk and back again that day. It was a pathetic little service with no hymns, but I can't remember anything except walking in holding Nicholas's hand with Richard in front with Andrew. While standing by the grave, Richard asked if he could see Freddie. Neither of the boys seemed to know what was going on, but I am glad they were there, even though my mother-in-law perhaps felt they should have been left at home. However, I had been excluded from my mother's funeral when I was five, and for a long time hoped her death was a lie and that she was still alive somewhere.

When the burial was over, I thought, thank goodness I can go home and see Freddie now. Friends and family came back to lunch. It was all quite jolly and I felt as if it were happening to someone else. I hated the idea that he died in January and would be so cold in his grave. It really upset me, though logically I knew it made no difference. Later, the four of us went back to the grave to see the flowers. So many people had sent them; it was really kind. I much preferred the ones that were sent to the funeral to the ones that came to the house – it was all too soon after the flowers I had received to celebrate his birth. One arrangement was identical to one I had received six weeks before – I nearly threw them out. One poor girl sent some beautiful freesias, which were meant to be congratulations, but arrived a few days after he died. I know she was mortified.

The physical pain of grief surprised me. There seemed to be a hole in my chest as if a part of me had been torn out. My arms ached to hold him again. I was slightly comforted by the idea that I made a little home for him just above my left breast, and even though physically dead, he would live on in me.

Among the many letters we received was one from a woman we had never met. Her son, Rupert, had suffered a cot death seventeen years earlier and she wrote, saying that she loved him as much now as when she had him. The idea seemed to make it less final, and I totally agree. I love Freddie as much now as when he died. He is still part of me and I think of him every day. Thinking of him like that helps with the fact that having lost a child you have lost not only the present but the future.

It is difficult to remember all the initial emotions. There was certainly anger. I was angry with Andrew for not having wanted or loved him like I did. Because of that, our short time together was not the happiest. But Andrew had been keeping his distance partly because there was a crisis at work and he was fantastically busy. I was angry with Freddie – how could he just give up and die? It was the time when there were all those Romanian orphans in the news – starving and uncared-for babies. They had survived and yet Freddie, who was so loved, had just decided life was not worth living. There was the feeling that it was not fair. As I had lost my mother so young, and my father was dead too, I had assumed that nothing would happen to my own children. Enormous pain and grief could suddenly hit me for no particular reason, or be set off by something obvious. There was anger and jealousy at all those women whose babies had survived. One of the worst times was when one of my greatest friends had her third child, a little girl, a few weeks later. I went to visit them, and held her, but I felt devastated and her mother knew how difficult it was. To this day I have not held another baby because I am terrified that if anything happened it would be somehow my fault.

People wrote wonderful letters. One person sent the words about footprints in the sand and God carrying them in times of trouble. The idea is beautiful but, if anything, Freddie's death made me even less of a believer than before. I gained no comfort from religion whatsoever. After the funeral there was no contact from the vicar. I understand this is not how it is in the Catholic Church. Perhaps it would have been better.

I spoke a lot to a friend who had lost her little girl the year before. It was wonderful to talk to Helen, knowing she too had gone through all the emotions. The Cot Death Helpline was excellent; talking to a stranger meant it was possible to say anything, including expressing my negative thoughts. A part of me blamed myself, and felt perhaps I had not loved him enough or could have done something to prevent it happening. I suspect there will always be 'if onlys'.

Over the first months there was total exhaustion – even the smallest thing seemed incredibly difficult. Each night before going to sleep I would rerun in my head the day Freddie died – as time went by I would include more details. Someone said nature lets you take in only a little at a time. I think if reality had hit me all in one it would have broken me. I grieved on my own and definitely shut Andrew out. It was only when he became ill and stressed that we did talk about it, but possibly it was too late. Certainly Freddie's death had a huge effect on Andrew, although he has had difficulty acknowledging it. When Andrew first became ill, he denied that it had anything to do with Freddie. When I went down with chronic active hepatitis, a disease of the immune system, I felt it must be linked to losing Freddie and the result of what grief had done to my body.

One of the things that helped me most was talking about Freddie and his death. My friends, without exception, listened uncomplainingly, which was, and is, wonderful. Even now I am grateful when someone mentions him. Veronica always remembers his birthday and the day he died. People gave us shrubs and trees in his memory. My sister-in-law Colette always has time to listen and comfort. It has been good remembering people's kindness. I do not see any sign of Richard and Nicholas being too affected by losing Freddie, and they mention him from time to time. They come with us to the grave on the anniversaries of his birth and death, but do not get upset.

After some months, Andrew and I discussed the possibility of having another baby. Andrew left the decision to me but was supportive. I became pregnant immediately, but then miscarried at fifteen weeks, after going through the usual nausea. Losing that baby – another boy – was virtually painless compared with what had happened with Freddie, and my main feeling was that someone, somewhere, felt that two children was enough. It was after this I got the hepatitis and had to go on steroids, which complicates pregnancy, so then was sterilised. It was a relief as I could no longer dither about having babies, though there was a certain amount of pressure to have another to heal the pain. Perhaps that would have made it easier.

Anne Diamond did wonders to publicise cot deaths and I am sure she has saved many lives. When Freddie died, my mother-in-law had never heard of a cot death. However, when all the new theories are in the press it can be hard. The 'at risk' babies are those who were premature, small at birth and born to smoking parents. Freddie was overdue by at least a week, weighed nearly 9 pounds and neither Andrew nor I smoked. I still wonder why Freddie had to die and what I had done to deserve his death. The theory that only those who can cope are given trials makes me angry. You have to cope: there is no choice if you have a husband and other children. It sounds trite, but time was the great healer, and the only way to distance the pain.

I am not sure Freddie's death changed me. It certainly did not make me a nicer person. I would like to think I am more understanding, but fear I am just less patient and more self-obsessed. Possibly I did learn what is important. One negative thing is that I am much more aware of what can go wrong – the thin line between life and death. Freddie's death was like turning off a light switch.

I have lost the inner faith that things will go well, and am more fearful for my other children. I mind desperately about seat belts in cars and other safety features.

I am not sure how much our marriage was affected. Neither of us is a great communicator. However, I think we are mainly at peace about Freddie now. It is pathetic he died so young, as Andrew would have loved him just as he does the others, given time. Our original disagreement about whether to have a third child has been a problem. We keep our emotional distance but we probably would have done that anyway.

Freddie would now be six, and it is odd to think how different our life would be. He smiled at me only once, that beautiful whole-hearted baby smile. I remember it so clearly, and the feeling and smell of him. I have kept the dress I was wearing when he died and it still has the milky stains on it. One comfort is that he did not suffer.

However painful Freddie's life and death were, given the choice I would go through it again. I have never, for one instant, regretted his short life.

Acknowledgements

To Richard, Jaime, Nicholas, Benj and Henry for giving me the space over ten weeks in lockdown 2020 to write it. To Mel Houldsworth for her encouragement and telling Lorne Forsyth about it. To my brother Mark, a proper writer, for his advice and good sense throughout it all.

But mostly to Lorne, without whom it would never have happened, and his Elliott & Thompson colleagues, Pippa Crane, Sarah Rigby and Simon Spanton-Walker, for their patient advice and endless good humour in dealing with an often grumpy novice.

ABOUT THE AUTHOR

Andrew Douglas-Home has lived on the banks of the River Tweed for most of his life. He was awarded an OBE in 2012 for his services to fishing and Scottish culture, recognising his long work helping to secure the environment of the Tweed River as well as for the role he played with the Abbotsford Trust in preserving Abbotsford House, the home and legacy of Sir Walter Scott. He was a Tweed Commissioner for over 35 years, acting as Chairman of the River Tweed Commission and Tweed Foundation for eight years between 2004 and 2012. He is, of course, a keen fisherman.